T0318282

It is hard to imagine a time when the world is more in need of new ideas. Almost overnight, it seems, long-held certainties have been swept away. Nothing can any longer be taken for granted. All nations are being tested, but probably none more than small island states, invariably surviving on a slender economic base. What will they do if tourism can no longer bring in much-needed income?

Peter Rudge's book could not be more timely. He knows about small island states – but he also understands the potential of the digital-creative industries. How, he asks, can the one help the other? Can we see these activities as a source of new energy and innovation? His answers are perceptive and stimulating. The book is a 'must' for all who are trying to make sense of the future. We should be more optimistic, if only because the seeds of sustainable change have already been planted. Now let us help them to grow.

Emeritus Professor Dennis Hardy, former Vice Chancellor
of the University of the Seychelles

Peter Rudge addresses a question that Small Island Developing States have been asking themselves (and others) for many years: what can we do to diversify our economy so that the precariousness resulting from over-dependence on tourism (or another single sector) can be removed?

The sheer importance of this question can be fully appreciated with the onslaught of the global COVID-19 pandemic at the beginning of 2020. Those countries that built their economies on tourism, for example, never thought that they would see a day when it would be necessary to close their borders to all incoming tourists. C-19 made it a reality. There was zero income from tourism for at least a quarter and economies collapsed.

Peter's discussion about diversification of SIDS economies into digital-creative industries offers policy makers inspiring ideas that hold real potential for the development of alternative development strategies.

For politicians and policy makers alike, as well as for academics and students of development policy, this book offers ideas that can be developed and embodied into national development strategies and upon which further research could follow.

Professor Fazeel Najeeb, Maldives National University, and former
Governor of the Central Bank of the Maldives and Maldives
Governor to the International Monetary Fund

Sustainable economic growth for Small Island Developing States (SIDS) provides the focus for this book. SIDS are introduced – islands where reliance on the Blue Economy has historically been the norm and where livelihoods are provided for through traditional industries like fishing and tourism. These are islands which have low carbon emissions yet which, ironically, are the most likely to suffer from climatic change and external forces that reveal vulnerabilities and result in shock.

The discussion regarding vulnerability and shock revolves around economic and climatic and environmental issues as well as cultural, societal and political changes. The discussion of this highlights the negative impact on SIDS in context of their economies through, for example, a collapse in the tourism industry and other island industries that rely on the Blue Economy and the consequential effect on food security and infrastructure, employment and income. This draws out the stark reality of macro-level external forces that have direct and indirect impact at meso-level and micro-level SIDS socio-economic systems.

The issue of regional and multi-regional collaboration in response to addressing low resilience, vulnerability and shock is raised, as is the role of cross-sector and multi-sector approaches to Blue Economy innovation. The emphasis on this is well-placed and sets the scene for the discussion in later chapters that focuses on a number of very relevant contemporary perspectives: creative industries and Sustainable Development Goals (SDGs), SIDS and the Fourth Industrial Revolution (4IR), the concept of clusters as a method for growing industrial sectors, a collaborative model for industry, academia and government, the orchestration of ecosystem development, entrepreneurship in SIDS and the digital-creative future.

The book presents an interesting narrative and discussion that forms a coherent and meaningful link and congruence between Small Island Developing States that have historically relied on natural local resources and ecosystems intrinsic to the Blue Economy and a forward-looking vision and approach based on collaborative innovation, research and policy to deliver equitable and sustainable economic growth for those islands in the face of the expanding digital, knowledge, service and experience economies. This latter aspect demonstrates the timely publication of this book – a time in which digital transformation is creating a new wave of change, altering human engagement and experience with the environment and creating new ecosystems and business models that are driving international trade and export of digital and physical assets.

The book offers a refreshing and contemporary approach to discussing the evolutionary and revolutionary force of digital innovation and transformation in the creative industries in the context of Small Island Developing States (SIDS). It includes facts and insights into the flow of resources, knowledge and skills capability, a UK-based case study and a discussion on creative industries and digital innovation and technologies in a distinct SIDS socio-economic non-urban context.

The content is well-researched, written in a clear, logical and coherent manner and will enable readers of this book – policy makers, practitioners, scholars and students of the subject area – to form a well-grounded and balanced view of the historic SIDS context and future opportunities that go beyond reliance on the Blue Economy.

Professor Khawar Hameed, Professor of Digital Innovation,
Birmingham City University

Beyond the Blue Economy

This book argues for a broader approach to sustainable growth in Small Island Developing States (SIDS).

Small island states such as those in the Caribbean, Indian Ocean and South Pacific face significant and growing threats from climate change, increasing political and social volatility, and rapidly evolving global trends in technology and tourism. Based on ten years of research, this book looks beyond the Blue Economy of tourism and fisheries and provides a model of how creative industries, innovation networks, creative clusters and digital transformation can give SIDS the foundation for a strong sustainable future. The book provides not only insights into how these emerging digital-creative sectors can drive developing economies but also actionable tools for policy makers, entrepreneurs and academics to deliver increased performance on the United Nations Sustainable Development Goals and, ultimately, growth and sustainability.

This book will be of great interest to scholars and practitioners of economic geography, sustainable development, development studies and the creative industries.

Peter Rudge is an award-winning creative entrepreneur, speaker, academic, writer and film and television producer. In 2018 he was named in the Creative England CE50 top 50 leaders and innovators in the digital-creative industries and is Founder and Chair of the Platform Moving Image Cluster in the UK. He is a fellow of the Royal Society of Arts, a member of the World Economic Forum's Expert Network, part of the United Nations Expert Group on Creative Economies and a UK representative to the World Business Angels Forum, where he sits on the Global Startup Committee.

Routledge Studies in Sustainable Development

This series uniquely brings together original and cutting-edge research on sustainable development. The books in this series tackle difficult and important issues in sustainable development including: values and ethics; sustainability in higher education; climate compatible development; resilience; capitalism and de-growth; sustainable urban development; gender and participation; and well-being.

Drawing on a wide range of disciplines, the series promotes interdisciplinary research for an international readership. The series was recommended in the *Guardian*'s suggested reads on development and the environment.

Achieving the Sustainable Development Goals
Global Governance Challenges
Edited by Simon Dalby, Susan Horton and Rianne Mahon, with Diana Thomaz

The Age of Sustainability
Just Transitions in a Complex World
Mark Swilling

A New World-System
From Chaos to Sustainability
Donald G. Reid

Buen Vivir as an Alternative to Sustainable Development
Lessons from Ecuador
Natasha Chassagne

Beyond the Blue Economy
Creative Industries and Sustainable Development in Small Island Developing States
Peter Rudge

For more information about this series, please visit: www.routledge.com

Beyond the Blue Economy

Creative Industries and Sustainable
Development in Small Island
Developing States

Peter Rudge

Routledge
Taylor & Francis Group

LONDON AND NEW YORK

First published 2021
by Routledge
2 Park Square, Milton Park, Abingdon, Oxon OX14 4RN

and by Routledge
52 Vanderbilt Avenue, New York, NY 10017

Routledge is an imprint of the Taylor & Francis Group, an informa business

© 2021 Peter Rudge

British Library Cataloguing-in-Publication Data
A catalogue record for this book is available from the British Library

Library of Congress Cataloging-in-Publication Data
A catalog record for this book has been requested

ISBN: 978-0-367-82025-1 (hbk)
ISBN: 978-0-367-75689-5 (pbk)
ISBN: 978-1-003-01151-4 (ebk)

Typeset in Times New Roman
by Apex CoVantage, LLC

Contents

Figures

Preface

There are 65 million people spanning across 58 countries that are bound by unique challenges and opportunities that no one else in the world can quite understand. Whilst Small Island Developing States (SIDS) across the globe are distinct from each other, they collectively experience both the burden and opportunity of common characteristics – vast ocean territories, geographic remoteness, low-lying land area, massive tourism sectors and rich biodiversity, to name a few.

These commonalities pose serious challenges to SIDS, encouraging a reliance on foreign energy and food imports as well as a particular vulnerability to climate change, which has engendered a loss of US$ 153 billion due to weather, climate and water-related hazards since 1970. However, they are also SIDS' greatest source of strength, presenting transformative opportunities for growth – opportunities that they have already demonstrated a commitment to fostering. In fact, island leaders have shown the world a profound example of leadership in climate action and the Blue Economy including expanding marine conservation, setting ambitious energy targets among others.

SIDS see their opportunity to become incubators of innovation. As small states with the will to shift old paradigms of development, they have the potential to leapfrog, boosting their digital transformation to pioneer innovative models and solutions with the potential for replication and up-scaling. With digital transformation comes the possibility to expand an underdeveloped sector – digital-creative industries – that can be a vehicle for preserving cultural heritage and accelerating sustainable development. As a vastly growing sector, SIDS can tap into this emerging area, as a means to diversify their tourism-reliant economies and safeguard their cultural integrity.

This proven potential for development should not be ignored, and our job as development workers is simply to support them in their journey there – enabling finance, advising on strategy and maximising investment. Local and indigenous communities are actively safeguarding 80% of the world's biodiversity but are too frequently left unconsulted in development scenarios. In SIDS, they offer a deep well of knowledge in how to best manage natural resources. In a similar vein, local governments are actively seeking and designating investment for climate resilience, building adaptive infrastructure and not least enabling digital transformation.

However, SIDS are running a race in which there are few moments to catch one's breath. The Covid-19 pandemic of 2020 has devastated their tourism industries, almost completely interrupting a sector that welcomed 44 million visitors in 2019 and accounts for nearly 30% of their GDP. The sector is a driver of development in SIDS, employing millions and serving as an important source for servicing many SIDS' heavy debt burdens. The macroeconomic impact of this drastic decline in tourism will require immense resources to recover from. Meanwhile, the crisis of climate change continues to snowball, and although they themselves account for only about 1% of global greenhouse gas emissions, SIDS continue to bear the brunt of climate events.

It is true; right now, SIDS face unprecedented barriers to realising their ambitions. But their propensity for change is equally unique. We are witnessing a moment of pivoting among SIDS across the world, which are transforming their vulnerabilities into opportunities – invigorating their marine industries with sustainable practices and digitised commerce, fostering energy independence through renewables, reimagining tourism as a tool for growth and ecological conservation and leaping into the digital era including expanding capacity for inclusive connectivity, creativity and entrepreneurialism. Furthermore, SIDS are emphasising multilateralism as a necessity for effective change.

These small states maintain a noteworthy presence on the world stage by demonstrating their strength and determination to not only overcome their vulnerabilities but transform them to their advantage. The opportunities opened up by the digital-creative sectors are no longer just confined to the developed world and offer a route for island communities to connect to these huge global markets, build resilience and celebrate their creative spirit.

SIDS represent 20% of the United Nations General Assembly; the future prosperity of the global community depends on the survival of island states. SIDS feel the urgency of action intimately and are anticipating the accelerating changes of the world around them, carving out a path for development that will safeguard their island futures and catalyse transformative change. The importance of this book, in highlighting the largely unexplored opportunities of the creative technology sectors in SIDS, lies in the compelling roadmap it puts forward for island states to achieve that resilient future.

Riad Meddeb
Senior Principal Advisor for Small Island Developing States
at the United Nations Development Programme

Acknowledgements

There are a number of people who have played a variety of important roles in the research and writing of this book, and of supporting this work more broadly.

I would like to thank Riad Meddeb, the Senior Principal Advisor for Small Island Developing States at the United Nations Development Programme, firstly for agreeing to write the preface for this book and secondly for his support of the concepts and ambitions outline here.

I would like to thank Professor Fazeel Najeeb of the Maldives National University, Dennis Hardy, Emeritus Professor at the University of the Seychelles, and Penda Choppy, Director of the Creole Language and Culture Research Institute at the same university, for their expert insights and help in conducting interviews during the period of the Covid-19 pandemic.

Many thanks as well go to Professor Khawar Hameed at Birmingham City University in the UK for his generous and expert insights into the impacts of digital transformation and the technologies of the Fourth Industrial Revolution.

I would like to thank Deb Rudge for sharing her knowledge and many years of experience leading cluster organisations and her insights into the expanded role of clusters outside major cities.

I would also like to thank my friends and colleagues in the Caribbean, particularly Sobers Esprit at the Competitive Business Unit of the Organisation of Eastern Caribbean States and St Lucian film producer and founder of the Caribbean Youth Film Festival, Colin Weekes, again for their help in gathering interviews and data during a particularly difficult and challenging time.

A special thank you must go to Dr. Keith Nurse, President/Principal of the Sir Arthur Lewis Community College in St Lucia for his long-standing work and research in promoting the creative industries in Small Island Developing States. His work provided some significant insights into the creative economies of the Caribbean.

Finally, I would like to thank Professor Martin Jones, Deputy Vice Chancellor at Staffordshire University, not only for his support and guidance but also for his book *Cities and Regions in Crisis: The Political Economy of Sub-National Economic Development* (2019) that acted as an inspiration and an exemplar for my own work.

Introduction

The decade of action in
the new normal

This book sets out to examine the potential for the creative and cultural industries to play a key role in the sustainable development of Small Island Developing States (SIDS) and to suggest both a practical and a theoretical approach to achieving this. It is framed by the notion that working towards the United Nations Sustainable Development Goals (SDGs) during this 'decade of action' requires a far more inclusive, multilateral and cross-sector approach than we have seen so far, in terms of policy, strategy, theory and, most crucially, implementation.

The book seeks to position the digital-creative industries as central to a more sustainable economy for SIDS, both in terms of the specifics of developing creative economies and in understanding the impact that a strong creative sector has on innovation and entrepreneurship across all sections of industry, society and culture.

Whilst this research has been conducted over an almost ten-year period, it has come into sharp focus in the early months of 2020. I am at home writing this book at the height of the Covid-19 pandemic, watching the impact on lives, jobs and economies around the world.

For SIDS, this impact is devastating. For a country like the Maldives, tourism directly contributes around 38% of its GDP, with the wider contribution being significantly more, and employs nearly 33% of the population. Whilst the financial crash of 2008 saw luxury tourism decline dramatically, having a significant negative impact on the Maldives economy, this pandemic has seen it stop completely (World Bank, 2020).

Public debt was already at around 59% of GDP in 2018, and according to the World Bank–IMF debt sustainability analysis (World Bank/IMF, 2019), Maldives was at high risk of debt distress then, with particular emphasis placed on the risks of fiscal slippage and a decline in tourism. That has now come to pass, and the effect of the collapse of the tourist market in the first quarter of 2020 on this debt risk cannot be overstated. The Maldives is not alone, and this economic situation is replicated across many island states.

Barbados' tourism sector contributed 44.1% or US$2.9 billion to GDP and provided 76,000 jobs in 2018 (World Travel and Trade Council, 2018). In October 2019, Barbados announced that it had reached a deal with its international market creditors, some 18 months after defaulting. That new repayment deal is now under serious threat just as Barbados was moving to re-establishing its debt sustainability. It is now facing a significant recession and given its place as the most economically stable and successful of the Eastern Caribbean islands, the outlook for the rest of the region is grim.

A broadening of SIDS economies then is now more important and urgent than ever, with the digital-creative, knowledge economy being front and centre as we look to recover from this global recession over the next few years. The arguments presented in this book then seem to have become even more pertinent than when I started writing in the autumn of 2019.

In the face of a collapse of the tourist market, the temptation of course is to double down on efforts to expand the Blue Economy, to increase activity in the sectors that make up that economy in a response to the hit to foreign revenues. There are significant dangers, however, for global ocean habitats in moving to increase the exploitation of that resource to offset the negative impacts of tourism declines.

The increased activity around ocean-floor mining, the developments of large-scale seaports and the growing amount of sea-born shipping are all part of the Blue Economy and all add to the accelerating degradation of ocean environments. The concept of the Blue Economy as a sustainable exploitation of this resource is all well and good, but there is a simple equation in play here that well-intentioned strategies do not alter. The more a resource is exploited the more it is negatively impacted, however much we try and implement sustainable methods, and in reality, there is a significant gap between Blue Economy theory and Blue Economy practice.

However, marine resources provide developing countries, particularly least developed countries (LDCs), with opportunities for growth through export earnings and support the livelihood of millions of people. Restricting exploitative ocean activities without first providing technical, financial and educational support to these countries to build other economic sectors is potentially damaging to those livelihoods.

Bhattacharya (2017) makes the important point that the present Blue Economy discourse could have significant negative impacts on developing countries unless effective special and differential treatment provisions are put in place.

Ultimately then, sustainable development in developing countries is a balancing act of numerous elements. As the Blue Economy is central to the prosperity of SIDS and if ocean degradation is to be halted and ultimately reversed, then we have to consider all the options available to developing sustainable island economies. Just looking to make traditional economic sectors – fishing and tourism, for example – more sustainable misses out on the growth opportunities of other equally valuable emerging sectors, such as those of the digital and creative economies.

As the world recovers from the pandemic and the deepest recession since the 1930s, there is a real danger of exploiting what is easily at hand for these island states and thereby undermining the very premise behind the Blue Economy.

So the argument put forward in this book is not just that SIDS should develop their creative industries as part of a broadening of SIDS' economic bases but that these digital, creative, knowledge-based sectors offer the best route of supporting a Blue Economy to be truly sustainable by taking the pressure of it to deliver. Alongside this, they are also key to developing a more active and inclusive innovation ecosystem, something that will be essential across all sectors, government departments and communities (Innocenti & Lazzeretti, 2019).

Economies are, just like the oceans, complex and fragile ecosystems. It is essential then that in all our discussions around working towards the SGDs and making SIDS truly sustainable, we do not think in the limited and siloed ways that we have so far. A much greater emphasis must be placed on cross-sector impacts, their ability to support and benefit each other, and the mechanisms we can put in place to facilitate collaborative innovation.

A difficult decade ahead

The early stages of delivering on the mission of the SDGs have been difficult, and whilst there have been some successes, we have also seen some areas going backwards. If we want to deliver a more sustainable, equitable, inclusive and prosperous society, then we have to innovate in ways that we have not done before.

This has never been more necessary now as we start the recovery from the Covid-19 pandemic, struggle to lessen the impacts of the deepest global recession since the 1930s and make good on the SDGs 'Decade of Delivery'. For SIDS, the SDGs are central to their prosperity, security and social and cultural coherence. It is essential to look beyond the traditional approaches and innovation methods if we are to make these regions and communities safe and sustainable.

In particular, we have to look beyond the narratives surrounding SIDS, their vulnerabilities and their opportunities. Building policy and strategy on outdated concepts, research and restrictive thinking will limit the impact that real innovators and entrepreneurs can deliver.

These countries provide a microcosm of the SDG agenda and delivery strategy – climate, spatially inclusive development, technology implementation, greater gender equality and food security, for example – so partnerships and collaborative working has to be a strategic focus for these regions.

Ultimately, the SDGs will be delivered not by governments but by ordinary people in the choices they make in their everyday lives. Governments can set frameworks and policy, but if these do not work for individuals and communities, then they will fail. The assumption that the SDGs just need the right legislation in place to make them happen is mistaken, so engaging the private sector and encouraging private capital and people-centred impact investment are essential.

We saw how the approach to the Millennium Development Goals, with a strongly government-focused, top-down strategy, failed to appreciate the need to fully engage the private sector, and whilst it did make some inroads around extreme poverty reduction and child mortality, criticism of the MDGs is not hard to find (Mishra, 2004; Oya, 2011; Barnes & Brown, 2011; Hayman, 2007).

The lack of engagement with the private sector at the time of setting the MDG agenda has been recognised now as problematic and has been addressed by all parties in the approach to the SDGs. The public–private partnership model though needs to be flexible as a one-size-fits-all approach does not work. The role of private sector innovation and entrepreneurship will vary dependent on location and local governance but is essential to be developed, encouraged and grown.

It is important though to not see private sector involvement as just access to investment and finance. Many of the discussions and proposed partnerships focus on this aspect, to the detriment of the real value that the private sector can bring. Private sector finance of course is essential, and we have seen the very positive innovations in green/blue bond financing and SDG bond financing such as those in the Seychelles (World Bank, 2018). The move of the corporations to adopt sustainable practices and to measure and communicate this through sustainability reporting is also important.

However, innovation and entrepreneurship are arguably the mechanisms whereby the SDGs will, in reality, be delivered, with specialised and local-ised finance, networks, skills development and education coming together with increased investment flows – both public and private.

It is also often the case that in policy and strategy meetings to discuss the role of the private sector in the SDGs, it is larger national and multinational corpora-tions that are to the fore. The private sector, however, is not a heterogeneous body. Small- and medium-sized enterprises (SMEs), entrepreneurs and start-ups, small-holder farms, cooperatives and social enterprises are all part of this and will be an essential element to achieving the goals and, in particular, building the prosperity and resilience of SIDS.

Alongside the increased private sector involvement, it is vitally important for SIDS and the developing world more widely to have a greater voice and a greater stakeholding in both innovating and implementing SDGs on the ground. It is local leadership that understands local networks, issues and opportunities that will provide perhaps an invigorated global leadership, looking beyond the traditional voices of the G7 or G20. These local conditions and local actors are often sidelined in the top-down, high-level, multilateral methodologies around SDG implementation.

The key to moving private sector participation in the SDGs is the realisation that there doesn't have to be a trade-off between economic growth and profitable business on the one hand and environmental protection and sustainability on the other. It is about the mix of sectors and the ability to enable knowledge-based innovation across sectors. Green growth, in its broadest sense, is about investing in low-carbon industries but now looking beyond what is normally thought of as green finance. It is far more than just clean energy, electric vehicles and smart-city public transport infrastructure.

These sectors though, and the all-important networks central to digital-creative industry development, are difficult to establish and manage given the nature of the geography and dispersed populations of many SIDS. This has inevitably restricted collaborative creation and innovation – something that is central to a successful creative industries sector. The research that underpinned the Platform cluster in the UK and the construction of a dispersed, polycentric and mobile-hub approach to building that ecosystem, however, holds some important lessons for SIDS regions such as the Eastern Caribbean or Indian Ocean, and these are discussed in later chapters.

It is crucial then that this new digital-creative economy is recognised in the strategy and policy development of governments, NGOs and multi-state organisations. Without that recognition and understanding, innovation in sustainable development for small island states will be severely restricted.

It is important that the narrative of vulnerability does not limit what these small island states and its people can achieve. Vulnerability is not an absolute nor a constant.

Digital transformation and the rise of the creative industries

Creative activities have always been a central part of human existence, of social and economic development and of our understanding of ourselves as individuals and communities.

There are many discussions on the nature of creativity, on the creative industries themselves and on the various classifications of what makes up the creative and cultural sector, so going over that here is not necessary. I do however want to look at how the creative industries have transformed and become truly economically ubiquitous.

This ubiquity has come about through the development and proliferation of digital technologies. The lowering costs and increasing performance of the technologies of production and distribution have democratised the creative content industries, transforming them from what was often an elitist profession to one where literally billions of people across the globe can produce and monetise their creativity.

The digital transformation of the whole of society and commerce has seen impacts extended from its traditional home of manufacturing, healthcare, construction and so on to most notably the cultural and creative industries. This has connected those industries to every other sector in a radical way. Take, for instance, the use of augmented reality in healthcare and construction or the impact of digital content marketing on tourism.

This digital transformation of the creative industries has also seen the creative transformation of the technology industries, with content production and distribution driving the technological innovation and market penetration of digital devices. It has also seen an explosion in the popularity and importance of education for these sectors in the developed world.

For SIDS however, creative industries education, particularly at the tertiary level, is severely limited and often very basic, undermining the ability of these nations to develop the pipeline of education, through innovation, to start-up and then to scale-up for young people on those islands. Without that pipeline of skills, creating a critical mass of creators and innovators, whether on specific islands or across island regions, becomes problematic.

This can partly be addressed by recognising that the advances in technology that the Fourth Industrial Revolution (4IR) can deliver need not be restricted to existing sectors. All too often though, research, strategy and government policy concentrate on the impact of these technologies on traditional industries. What technologies such as blockchain, 5G, artificial intelligence (AI) and machine learning (ML) can do for SIDS is open up new commercial opportunities beyond those already established.

These technologies will have a significant impact on Blue Economy, but it is also important not to realise that small island states can benefit from innovation beyond just tourism or aquaculture, for example.

The transformation of the creative and cultural industries by these emerging technologies has been truly radical. The production, distribution and monetisation of creative content and services are now no longer limited by geographical location. Digital cultural goods are by far the biggest revenue source for the digital economy and are the main driver for the sale of electronic goods. The ubiquity of mobile devices and the subsequent shift in content consumption to 'mobile first' is changing both the digital and creative economies. These two sectors are now so inextricably linked in a truly symbiotic relationship that the boundaries between them are disappearing.

The new technologies of the 4IR are increasing and further enabling these spillovers to such an extent that we can see the soft and hard innovation processes merging, with content production, distribution platform networks and technology device R&D becoming increasingly symbiotic.

Creativity and the creative industries then will increasingly be understood as a vital resource for every economic sector in every region. Restreppo and Marquez (2013) outline this process through a process of producing positive externalities in the form of knowledge, product and network spillovers.

It is important though to understand the difference between creativity and creative and cultural industries. Creativity has always been part of innovation in sectors such as engineering, medicine and science, but the creative industries have not. The digital technologies of the Third Industrial Revolution, and particularly those of the internet, production and distribution, have now seen the creative industries now permeating every economic sector.

The new 4IR technologies such as immersive content, blockchain and 5G are further transforming creative and cultural industries to such an extent that they are now central to many developed economies and seen as aspirational targets for many developing regions.

These opportunities are not just restricted to the traditional bases of creative industry production. Africa and the Middle East have the greatest opportunity to grow their creative economy, with currently only 1.1% of their GDP coming from these sectors, in comparison to around 3% for the rest of the world (UNESCO, 2018).

These industries can also become central pillars of sustainable production in developing regions through their ability to attract younger populations and to be highly productive. Worldwide, the creative and cultural sectors employ more people between the ages of 15 and 29 than any other sector and contribute more to GDP than an economy-wide average. Workers in the film and television sectors, for example, generate 78% more added value per worker than the rest of the economy in China and are twice as productive than the average in South Korea (Oxford Economics, 2011).

Orange is the new green (or Blue)

In 1989, the UK Government's Department for Environment, Food and Rural Affairs commissioned a group of leading environmental economists to advise the government on whether there was any consensus on a definition of the term 'sustainable development' and the implications of this on the measurement of economic progress. The report titled *Blueprint for a Green Economy* (Pearce et al., 1989) led the way for an international cooperative response to the crises of environmental degradation and economic need.

In 2008, the United Nations Environment Programme (UNEP) launched the Green Economy Initiative, aimed at providing policy support and analysis for carbon reduction across sectors and the building of green industries. The term has since become widespread and inspired the creation of the concept of the Blue Economy, introduced by Gunter Pauli in his 2010 book *The Blue Economy: 10 Years, 100 Innovations, 100 Million Jobs* (Pauli, 2010).

A year later, John Howkins coined the term 'Orange Economy' in his 2011 book (Howkins, 2011). The Orange Economy, as a descriptor of the creative and cultural industries as an economic force, is commonly used in the Caribbean and Latin American contexts and was further discussed and popularised by Buitrago and Duque (2013) as the focus of a report for the Inter-American Development Bank.

The Orange economy is yet to have the same prominence as the Green and Blue economies, and its role in the SDGs is limited at best. But it really shouldn't be. The Green and Blue economies have at their heart the concept of the sustainable use of natural resource, one land-based and the other water-based – in oceans, rivers and lakes.

The Orange economy and particularly the digital-creative sectors not only have little direct use of natural resource in the content production but also can have a truly transformative impact on innovation across every other economic and social sector. Traditionally and in many cases this is still perpetuated; innovation has been coupled both conceptually and practically to science and technology – its value seen in hard outputs.

What is often missed in discussions of the creative and cultural economies are their contribution to the initiation and processes of innovation in its widest sense (Buitrago & Duque, 2013; Benavente & Grazzi, 2017).

The Orange or creative economy then has the potential to transform not just the sustainability of economies but their innovation capabilities. For SIDS looking to broaden their economies as well as to transform them with digital-creative and knowledge-based sectors, this is of critical importance.

One central aspect to this transformation though could be seen to impede that progress.

The need for creative economy data

Decision-making, whether at an individual, corporate, governmental or global level, is ultimately driven by contextualised data married to strategic direction. In a 2014 study of creative industries data, Oxford Economics (2014) produced a report for the Inter-American Development Bank and the British Council, examining the potential contribution of the creative and cultural sectors to the Americas. Out of the 45 countries researched, only five produced data to the required level of granularity, at four- or five-digit level, that is necessary for reliable analysis. This again brings into focus the perceptions of the importance of these industries in these regions. What there is tends to concentrate in large part on the cultural aspects of the sector, whether that's tangible or intangible heritage. Thirteen of the countries produced no creative industries data at all.

The data sets that are in existence are often fragmented and use disparate and sometimes contradictory methods that make analysis and contextualising particularly difficult. This absence unfortunately then leads to estimates based on historical data and theoretical discussions that simply review and reframe existing literature that is often distanced from commercial reality.

If the creative and cultural sectors are to play a central role in building resilience and economic stability in SIDS, and in delivering the 2030 Agenda more broadly, then supporting the research and creation of timely, applicable and impact-focused data has to be a priority.

Background to this research

This advocacy of the creative industries has come through a 30-year career in and around the creative sector, specifically the film and television industries, both in the UK and in Hollywood as a screenwriter, development executive with the major studios and independent producer.

Over the last ten years I have committed more time to supporting and mentoring young filmmakers and creative entrepreneurs in the UK and Eastern Caribbean, with the Platform cluster being the most concrete expression of that work. It is the nexus of the professional, academic and philanthropic work that has led to the writing of this book.

Through this work and my advocacy of the creative industries as a route to sustainable development, I have been honoured to become a member of the World Economic Forum's (WEF's) Expert Network and the United Nations Expert Group on Creative Economies.

I presented an overview of this research at the Expert Group meeting in Geneva in October 2019 and was part of the WEF's strategic intelligence briefing on development finance flows in April 2020. Both of these meetings demonstrated that there is still a considerable gap between the recognition of the importance of creative, knowledge-based economies and their implementation within strategy and policy on the ground.

There have been individual research and practice-based projects that have informed the individual chapters; for instance, the chapter on clusters was informed by the research behind the Platform Moving Image Cluster in Stoke on Trent and the effects of its launch and activity.

The work in St Lucia over a number of years has contributed significantly to the entrepreneurship and Triple Helix chapters, and I would like to acknowledge the support, both financial and logistical, of the Organisation of Eastern Caribbean States (OECS), the government of St Lucia, the Trade Export and Promotion Agency and the University of the West Indies. The dialogue I've had between government ministers and policy makers, multinational organisations such as the United Nations (UN) and specifically the United Nations Conference on Trade and Development (UNCTAD), the universities in many SIDS regions and the many creative entrepreneurs on the ground in the Caribbean, Indian Ocean and Pacific islands has been the backbone to the underpinning research.

The results of these discussions were revealing about the state of thinking around the digital-creative and cultural industries and the often unconscious culture of sectoral hegemony that exists within these various bodies.

Charlina Vitcheva, the director of smart and sustainable growth at the European Commission's Directorate-General, commented that many regional development plans lacked a real vision for transformation and were simply old, tired innovation strategies that had been repackaged (EU, 2015). This lack of vision also holds true for many of the projects, strategies and research papers that seek to 'transform' the sustainable development of SIDS – their focus simply a rework of the traditional oceans economy sector plans.

This book then seeks to present that 'real vision for transformation' by proposing a disruptive approach to the question of sustainable development for these island states through a transformation based on creative sectors and digital technology. The process was made more difficult due to the absence of reliable, up-to-date and comprehensive data on the global creative industries, and it is an issue that still needs to be addressed. For SIDS that data is virtually non-existent.

Examination of research, strategy and policy documents shows a common theme for proposed sustainable development, with traditional sectors such as tourism, fisheries and other maritime industries, and environmental issues being very much to the fore. The creative and cultural industries have very limited mention and when they do, it is closely aligned to cultural heritage, which misses the impact and opportunities of new technologies and digital exports.

Continuing this work more recently in the Indian Ocean shows similar challenges. For this region, however, those challenges are even greater, with a considerable gap in infrastructure, investment and level of activity between islands such as Seychelles and the Maldives and the Caribbean region.

Interestingly, the work done in establishing the Platform Moving Image Cluster in Stoke on Trent threw up some notable comparisons with these island nations and regions, and this is covered in the chapters on clusters beyond the city and ecosystems and orchestrators.

Although the similarities between the Seychelles and Stoke on Trent may not be obvious, they both struggle with the historical dominance of one industry sector and the polycentric nature of their geography. This allowed some theoretical musings to be tested out in observations and interviews with key stakeholders in both locations, firming up the concepts and arguments that led to the proposal of an Agile Helix.

Methodologies

The research behind these projects and ultimately this book then followed three principal methods. First was a literature survey that examined academic work, governmental and multinational strategies and reports from organisations such as the UN, the WEF, the National Endowment for Science, Technology and the Arts (NESTA) and the World Bank, along with specialist consultancies such as McKinsey, PricewaterhouseCoopers and Klynveld Peat Marwick Goerdeler (KPMG). Second was ethnographic research in the principal locations that included on-the-ground observations and interviews with practitioners, SMEs and national government departments.

Research on creative and cultural industries typically uses this mixture of mutually informing quantitative and qualitative methods (Currid & Connolly, 2008). This mixed methodology uses analysis of data sets and macro-patterns, questionnaires, semi-structured interviews and more ethnographically focused methods such as participant observation and individual case studies.

This ethnographic approach was particularly useful in the research for this book, with significant insights being gained from the informal time spent with individuals and companies over a number of years, in both the UK and the Caribbean, using relaxed networking as part of the research process (Power & Jansson, 2008).

These methods are particularly suitable for creative industries research where an understanding of the social, cultural and work environments allows for a consideration of 'place', so often seen as important to creative sector growth. These methods have been essential to this book's exploration of the complex interpersonal relations that operate within and that surround the creative and cultural industries in small island states.

Alongside this, it is important to recognise that whilst this methodological mix has clear value, there are dangers in relying simply on data points to inform policy making and strategic growth plans based on 'general conclusions about the cultural industries across disparate geographies' (Currid & Williams, 2009).

For example, the creative industries often trade on the relationship between the uniqueness of their products and the specific place-based identities that created them. It is important that we take 'place' seriously and marry this understanding to the quantitative and qualitative data gathered during any research. This goes beyond the idea of place-based product heritage and branding, however, as there are dangers in seeing places as simply associated with specific creative sectors, certain Caribbean islands, for instance, being associated primarily with carnivals.

Indeed, over-reliance on place-based heritage production often stifles the uptake of new creative industries, those based on digital technologies for example, in national or regional growth plans. So, rather than just seeing place as linked to a particular product, it is about a much wider social, economic, cultural and educational understanding of place.

We can then create tightly focused analyses of creative sectors in regions which are built on a rich mix of data, understanding and analysis.

I've noted the lack of reliable data on the creative and cultural industries, and this is particularly acute in researching the creative sector in small island states (Martinaityte & Kregzdaite, 2015). Data for world trade in creative products and services are difficult to obtain as many developing countries do not track and report on the creative and cultural industries as an important sector. Assumptions and estimates therefore have to be made (UNCTAD, 2018).

The choice of using an ethnographic approach then that focuses largely on embedding into local communities over a period of time is a methodological response to the problems of the scarcity of reliable or up-to-date quantitative data sources. This approach allowed an exploration of how creative and cultural industries were embedded in key social actors and their networks (Coe, 2000).

This field work was carried out in the Eastern Caribbean and Indian Ocean over a period of six years from 2014, working with young creative entrepreneurs, filmmakers, government ministries and regional organisations. This included workshops with SMEs, activities and talks to school classes, meetings and reports for government and non-governmental organisations and the observation of filmmakers on sets as part of a training programme.

Interviews with practitioners, academics and support agencies gave a picture of a fragmented industry that has huge potential but struggles with a number of crucial factors. These factors form a common thread of challenges for SIDS regions, even to some extent, in developed countries. This was notable in the research behind the establishment of Platform, the Moving Image Cluster for Stoke on Trent and Staffordshire. Research into the local digital-creative economy in this region was influential in the design of the later work in SIDS regions and had been conducted over a ten-year period from 2008.

New models and new approaches

In bringing this research together over the last few years and particularly in writing it in these extraordinary times, it became apparent that if SIDS were to benefit from the strengths and opportunities of the digital-creative economy and be delivered in the context of achieving the 2030 Agenda for the Sustainable Development Goals, that innovation was essential.

This innovation had to be not just in products and services, in technologies and applications but in the structures and mechanisms by which these innovations, connections and collaborations were to be engineered and implemented. Several chapters in this book then will suggest specific innovations that can positively impact the development and sustainability of digital-creative economies in SIDS.

In Chapter 4 I discuss how the application of clusters and creative hubs to the dispersed and polycentric nature of many SIDS and SIDS regions could work and suggest new models of dispersed clusters and moveable hubs.

In Chapter 5 I outline the concept of the Agile Helix as a solution to the restrictive and now rather outdated and confused ideas of the triple/quadruple/quintuple/ etc. helix models and examine how this can work in SIDS regions.

Chapter 6 looks at the need for creative economy ecosystems to be not only supported but also orchestrated and takes the concept of the creative city as part of the mechanism for doing this and applies it to SIDS to build the creative island.

Finally, in the Conclusion, 'Creative futures for Small Island Developing States', I suggest that to deliver the skills and attributes that will be needed for the digital-creative and 4IR era, a move away from the subject-based concepts of STEM/STEAM to a more skills and abilities-based approach is warranted. This is outlined as Creative, Critical and Cognitive – C3.

This final chapter also proposes the concept of the Second Creative Revolution, or 2CR, as a way of understanding the importance of the digital-creative sector over the last 25 years, as well as the central role it will play in delivering the SDGs.

This book then sets to not just examine and contextualise the research described previously but also propose a set of applicable and real-world concepts and innovations that can act as a framework for SIDS to build strong and sustainable creative economies.

References

Barnes, A. & Brown, G.W. 2011. The Idea of Partnership within the Millennium Development Goals: Context, Instrumentality and the Normative Demands of Partnership. *Third World Quarterly*, 32, pp. 165–180.

Benavente, J.M. & Grazzi, M. 2017. *Public Policies for Creativity and Innovation: Promoting the Orange Economy in Latin America and the Caribbean.* Inter-American Development Bank, Washington, DC.

Bhattacharya, S. 2017. Issues Relating to the Blue Economy. Viewpoint paper No.3 2017. Accessed at http//:cuts-international.org.

Buitrago Restreppo, F. & Duque Marquez, I. 2013. *The Orange Economy: An Infinite Opportunity*. Inter-American Development Bank, Washington, DC.

Coe, N.M. 2000. The View from Out West: Embeddedness, Inter-Personal Relations and the Development of an Indigenous Film Industry in Vancouver. *Geoforum*, 34(4), p. 390.

Cunningham, S. & Potts, J. 2015. Creative Industries and the Wider Economy. In *The Oxford Handbook of Creative Industries*, pp. 387–404. Oxford University Press, Oxford.

Currid, E. & Connolly, J. 2008. Patterns of Knowledge: The Geography of Advanced Services and the Case of Art and Culture. *Annals of the Association of American Geographers*, 98(2), pp. 414–434.

Currid, E. & Williams, S. 2009. The Geography of Buzz: Art, Culture and Milieu in Los Angeles and New York. *Journal of Economic Geography*, 10(3), p. 426.

European Union. 2015. *EU Smart Specialisation Conference*. EU, Riga.

Hayman, R. 2007. Are the MDGs Enough? Donor Perspectives and Recipient Visions of Education and Poverty Reduction in Rwanda. *International Journal of Educational Development*, 27, pp. 371–382.

Howkins, J. 2011. *The Creative Economy: How People Make Money from Ideas*. Penguin, London.

Innocenti, N. & Lazzeretti, L. 2019. Do the Creative Industries Support Growth and Innovation in the Wider Economy? Industry Relatedness and Employment Growth in Italy. *Industry and Innovation*, 26(10), pp. 1152–1173.

Martinaityte, W. & Kregzdaite, R. 2015. The Factors of Creative Industries Development in Nowadays Stage. *Economics and Society*, 8(1), pp. 56–71.

Mishra, U.S. 2004. Millennium Development Goals: Whose Goals and for Whom? *British Medical Journal*, 329, p. 742.

Oxford Economics. 2011. *The Economic Contribution of the Film and Television Industries in South Korea*. Oxford University Press, Oxford.

Oxford Economics. 2014. *The Economic Impact of the Creative Industries in the Americas*. Oxford Economics, Oxford.

Oya, C. 2011. Africa and the Millennium Development Goals (MDGs): What's Right, What's Wrong and What's Missing. *Revista De Economia Mundial*, 27, pp. 19–33.

Pauli, G. 2010. *The Blue Economy: 10 Years, 100 Innovations, 100 Million Jobs*. Paradigm Publications, Brookline, MA.

Pearce, D.W., Barbier, E.B. & Markandya, A. 1989. *Blueprint for a Green Economy*. Earthscan, London.

Power, D. & Jansson, J. 2008. Cyclical Clusters in Global Circuits: Overlapping Spaces in Furniture Trade Fairs. *Economic Geography*, 84(4), pp. 423–448.

UNCTAD. 2018. *Creative Economy Outlook: Trends in International Trade in Creative Industries*. UNCTAD, Geneva.

UNESCO. 2018. Re I Shaping Cultural Policies; Advancing Creativity for Development. Report on the Implementation of the UNESCO 2005 Convention on the Protection and Promotion of the Diversity of Cultural Expression. Accessed at http://en.unesco.org/global-report-2018.

World Bank. 2018. *Seychelles: Introducing the World's First Sovereign Blue Bond – Mobilising Private Sector Investment to Support the Ocean Economy*. World Bank, Washington, DC.

World Bank. 2020. Maldives Overview 2020. Accessed at http://worldbank.org/en/country/Maldives

World Bank/IMF. 2019. *Joint World Bank-IMF Debt Sustainability Analysis 2019*. World Bank, Washington, DC. Accessed at http://hdl.handle.net/10986/32580

World Travel and Trade Council. 2018. *Travel and Tourism Global Economic Impact and Issues, 2018*. WTTC, London.

1 The challenges of Small Island Developing States and the Blue Economy

Introduction

The challenges faced by countries around climate change, environmental degradation, rising population and inequality and global economic uncertainty are common. Nowhere do these challenges come into sharper focus though than in SIDS. Alongside the challenges mentioned, they deal with small, often dispersed populations, making public service delivery particularly difficult. They are often susceptible to devastating weather events and can struggle to recover from these due to narrow economies that rely heavily on the oceans for much of their GDP. That ocean-based or Blue Economy is at the heart of much of the discussion around building the strength and sustainability of these island economies, but that in itself faces some significant challenges.

This chapter will examine the specific challenges and vulnerabilities of SIDS, the challenges and problems with overemphasising the Blue Economy and the ways in which the digital-creative industries can aid in facing those challenges.

SIDS as a concept

SIDS were first recognised as a distinct group at the United Nations Conference on Environment and Development in June 1992, a group of island countries that displayed certain characteristics such as small size, limited resources and geographic dispersion. The Agenda 21 document at this conference recognised that these small island states were a special case for both environment and development.

The United Nations Department of Economic and Social Affairs (UN-DESA) currently recognises 57 SIDS (37 UN-Members and 20 Non-UN), divided into three main geographic areas:

1. Caribbean
2. Pacific
3. Atlantic, Indian Ocean, Mediterranean and South China Sea (AIMS).

Specifically, the World Bank defines small states as countries that (a) have a population of 1.5 million or less or (b) are members of the World Bank Group Small States Forum (World Bank, 2016).

They are, however, a diverse group with varying population sizes, cultural characteristics and development progress. Some island states, such as the Maldives, have officially become an upper-middle-income country and is classed by the World Bank as a development success (World Bank, 2020b) with the second-highest Human Development Index (HDI) rank in South Asia and an income per capita of $11,890.

In the same Indian Ocean region however, the Comoros has a per capita income of $1362, with 23.5% of the population living below the poverty line (World Bank, 2018). This diversity however does not mean that there are also some notable common characteristics, particularly as is generally stated, vulnerabilities, that SIDS share.

Key characteristics of SIDS

The Organisation for Economic Cooperation and Development (2018c) does state that the differences among SIDS "point to the need for tailored development approaches across the group", yet the common challenges they face mean there is "scope for mutual learning".

SIDS are often discussed in their regional subgroups – for example, the Pacific, the Caribbean and AIMS SIDS. However, it has also been suggested that some smaller SIDS subgroups could be created along issues-based categorisations (Alonso Rodriguez et al., 2014).

The most often cited defining characteristics and vulnerabilities of SIDS are their small population sizes, their remoteness from economic markets and principal trade routes, and their often dispersed populations. These dispersed populations mean that domestic markets are small, limiting the economies of scale that larger countries with more condensed populations benefit from (Bartelme et al., 2018). This dispersion also leads to high per-capita costs to deliver essential public services such as health, education and security, with a subsequent significant impact on public finances.

These 'negative effects' of small, dispersed populations and the remoteness from markets lead to "high production and trading costs, limiting investment, competitiveness and the scope for integrating global value chains" (Organisation for Economic Cooperation and Development, 2018b).

This coupling of limited domestic market size and higher export costs means that SIDS economies generally focus on a limited number of sectors, most notably tourism and fisheries, thereby fostering their narrow economic bases. Because of this, public sector jobs often account for a large percentage of the total employment on island states, with the Maldives, for example, having around 40% of its total employment in the public sector (World Bank, 2020c).

The public–private wage differentials along with the other benefits associated with public employment disincentivise young people from seeking private sector jobs and also hold down private entrepreneurship. This has caused relatively elevated levels of youth unemployment, at 15.3%, and low rates of women participating in the workforce (Organisation for Economic Cooperation and Development, 2018b).

This can lead to a shortage of skilled workers and, despite the high unemployment rate, a reliance then on expatriate labour. This stems from limited access to good-quality secondary, tertiary and vocational education, particularly away from capital cities and for those nations with archipelagic structures, coupled to a lack of high-skill and high-value jobs opportunities and the subsequent 'brain drain' of talent to larger population centres in other countries (de la Croix et al., 2014).

Vulnerability

Vulnerability is an all-consuming narrative for SIDS, an often top-line statement about these regions and unfortunately an all too regular justification for the quasi-colonial attitudes of many developed countries and international organisations.

Vulnerability is a pervasive and continuing narrative for SIDS, one that whilst undoubtedly true also can act as a hindrance to progressive and innovative thinking on regional development.

The concept of vulnerability combines the probability and impact of physical and economic hazardous events (vulnerability), with a particular country's ability to manage or adapt to that event (resilience), according to the Environmental Vulnerability Index (EVI) (Organisation for Economic Cooperation and Development, 2018c). The EVI is a measure of the vulnerability of developing countries to economic and environmental shocks, and the determinants of exposure to shocks (e.g. population size and remoteness) (Organisation for Economic Cooperation and Development, 2018c).

As an example, tropical storms and cyclones particularly affect SIDS not only due to their dispersed/remote geographies but also because their small economies and limited state capacity complicate policy responses to these events. This then has a negative impact not just on food security and infrastructure but also on employment and local incomes as these events can have very significant impacts on tourism, a key economic component of the majority of SIDS (Yamamoto & Esteban, 2014).

Climate vulnerabilities

SIDS are particularly vulnerable to the climate crisis and will continue to be among the earliest and most impacted countries (United Nations Office of the High Representative for the Least Developed Countries, Landlocked Countries and Small Island Developing States, 2015). This was officially identified in the Barbados Programme of Action for the Sustainable Development of SIDS in 1994 (United Nations Office of the High Representative for the Least Developed Countries, Landlocked Countries and Small Island Developing States, 2015).

> Their climate is influenced by large ocean-atmosphere interactions such as trade winds, El Niño, monsoons and tropical cyclones. With populations,

agricultural lands and infrastructures tending to be concentrated in the coastal zone, any rise in sea level will have significant and profound effects on settlements, living conditions and island economies.

(United Nations Office of the High Representative for the Least Developed Countries, Landlocked Countries and Small Island Developing States, 2015)

Changes in sea levels and their impact on coastal regions and livelihoods, ocean acidification and changing chemistry, changing weather patterns and ocean currents and temperatures, all have significant impacts on the whole of the Blue Economy.

The impact on aquaculture of changing ocean chemistry and temperature, affecting both the distribution and stock levels of fisheries and their supporting ecosystems, could be considerable. We see this very clearly in the coral bleaching that has, and continues to, destroyed large areas of coral reefs across the globe.

This reef destruction significantly impacts the level of tourism to SIDS regions, as we have seen from previous episodes of bleaching, such as in 2016, which was the longest and most significant event ever recorded (McDermott, 2016).

Many SIDS are characterised by low resilience to climate change, and the impact on their Blue Economy development will be considerable if collaborative action is not forthcoming. This is not only in terms of regional and multi-regional cooperation – which is well understood and accepted – but also in terms of cross-sector and multi-sector approaches to Blue Economy innovations that respond to those climate challenges and changes. This second point often goes unrecognised.

Responses to these changes are generally formed around mitigating the extent of climate change–adapting activities to take into account the changes already happening (Colgan, 2018).

Ironically, the contribution to global warming of SIDS is low in terms of total carbon emissions, although they are the most likely to suffer the adverse effects of climate change (Ponte et al., 2017).

Economic vulnerability

Most SIDS have narrowly based economies that depend on just a few products and sectors due to their small domestic markets, distance from markets, high production costs, limited competitiveness and difficulties in integrating in global value chains (Organisation for Economic Cooperation and Development, 2018b). This is especially evident in some of the LDCs that are SIDS (e.g. Guinea-Bissau, Timor-Leste, Kiribati, Vanuatu and Tuvalu) (Organisation for Economic Cooperation and Development, 2018b).

This lack of diversification in SIDS economies means that their domestic revenues can be erratic, particularly as their production bases are often concentrated in sectors that are vulnerable to external shocks – as we have seen with the impact of the Covid-19 pandemic on tourism – and are then at risk of large fluctuations in domestic and tax revenues.

In Timor-Leste for example, tax revenues accounted for 133% of GDP in 2012 but then fell to 40% in 2015 (Organisation for Economic Cooperation and Development, 2018a). This level of fluctuation makes government planning, particularly around long-term and large-scale infrastructural development, extremely difficult.

These narrow economic bases and volatile national revenues result in a difficult balancing act for SIDS governments – caught between the desire to develop levels of social, cultural, educational and physical infrastructure and the requirement to take on more national debt to achieve that.

The impact of that of course is that debt sustainability becomes a problem when any shock to the economic system occurs, such as we have seen with the loss of tourist revenue due to the Covid-19 pandemic. The ability to repay those debts impacts on creditworthiness, thus restricting access to capital markets and increasing the costs of any future borrowing.

In the Maldives for example, public debt was already at around 59% of GDP in 2018, and according to the World Bank-IMF debt sustainability analysis (World Bank/IMF, 2019), Maldives was at high risk of debt distress then, with particular emphasis placed on the risks of fiscal slippage and a decline in tourism. That has now come to pass and the effect of the collapse of the tourist market in the first quarter of 2020 on this debt risk cannot be overstated. The Maldives is not alone, and this economic situation is replicated across many island states.

Barbados' tourism sector contributed 44.1% or US$2.9 billion to GDP and provided 76,000 jobs in 2018 (World Travel and Trade Council, 2018). In October 2019, Barbados announced that it had reached a deal with its international market creditors, some 18 months after defaulting. That new repayment deal is now under serious threat just as Barbados was moving to re-establish its debt sustainability. It is now facing a significant recession and given its place as the most economically stable and successful of the Eastern Caribbean islands, the outlook for the rest of the region is grim.

The fact that SIDS also have relatively small domestic markets and are dependent on foreign markets and financing has traditionally made it difficult for other sectors to take up the slack of a tourism downturn. Briguglio (2014) highlights how their geographic isolation increases their economic vulnerability due to their strong dependence on narrow resources from the main world markets. It is these factors that make the development of digital, knowledge-based sectors in SIDS so vital now.

The issue of finance and debt

Many SIDS are classed as middle-income countries and as such become ineligible for Official Development Assistance (ODA). This has a particular effect on areas such as the financing of public infrastructure development and educational capacity-building, with the graduation from low to middle income also seeing the reduction of access to concessional finance from multilateral financial institutions. This then inevitably leads to large structural account deficits and when shocks such as the Covid-19 pandemic hit, debt vulnerabilities became all too real and obvious (Quak, 2019).

The Addis Ababa Action Agenda of the Third International Conference on Financing for Development (UN, 2015) identified a framework to support global sustainable development, including both domestic and international resources from both public and private finance.

SIDS have seen, on average, an increase in the debt to gross national income (GNI) ratios over the last 15 years, with the current average ratio of 57% being substantially higher than that of other developing countries, which stands at 47%.

With foreign direct investment (FDI) being volatile and susceptible to increasingly dynamic market forces, they can contribute little to SIDS sources of external finance, just 12% between 2012 and 2015. In fact, the majority of external finance for SIDS comes from their diaspora, which for the same period amounted to 52% (Organisation for Economic Cooperation and Development, 2018a).

Again, this source of external finance is particularly susceptible to economic shocks, as well as cultural, societal and political changes.

Concessional finance

Concessional finance can be an important source of funding for SIDS, but it is strongly concentrated on a very limited number of both providers and recipients and focused on a small number of projects. Over half (58%) of concessional finance reaching SIDS came from just five providers – Australia, the United States, the European Union, France and IDA (World Bank, 2016). So just as domestic revenues for SIDS are susceptible to external shocks and market factors, the level of concessional finance available is susceptible to shifts in the priorities and political policies of the main providers.

Concessional finance is also concentrated in a few regions and countries. In the period 2012–2015, SIDS in the Caribbean received 44% of all the concessional finance flows – around US$8.4 billion. Pacific SIDS received 42%, whilst SIDS in AIMS regions received just 14% (Organisation for Economic Cooperation and Development, 2018a). However, these regional allocations hide further disparities in the share of finance flows with Haiti and the Dominican Republic accounting for 64% of the total allocations to the Caribbean.

This concessional finance also tends to be very sector limited, with little if any focusing on the broadening of economic bases through the development of a stronger and more entrepreneurial private sector, better business environments and the consequent attraction of more private finance and FDI. Whilst many concessional finance flows are in response to natural and humanitarian disasters, there has to be an element of this that is proactive and not just responsive. At least a proportion of this finance has to be channelled towards interrupting the cycle of low growth and vulnerability that so often dominates the SIDS narrative.

For instance, finance is aimed at developing stronger domestic private sector activity, particularly where knowledge-based, creative and digitally focused

SMEs can break the dependence on a few exports that exacerbate the vulnerabilities that come with economic openness (Briguglio et al., 2009).

There has been a noticeable lack of knowledge-based, private sector involvement in discussions around finance for sustainable development in SIDS, with these actions being seen as primarily driven by governments and international agencies. It is important though that available finance, whether public, private or in combination, is used to build entrepreneurially focused policy and regulatory frameworks that can support a broader private sector beyond tourism and the wider Blue Economy–related sectors.

This is going to require some innovation in terms of the approaches to sustainable finance flows, government strategies and the frameworks put forward by the key international agencies. In a post-pandemic world however, this innovation is critical as reliance on the Blue Economy has been shown to be a significant weakness.

Reliance on the Blue Economy

The term 'Blue Economy' was introduced by Gunter Pauli in his 2010 book *The Blue Economy: 10 Years, 100 Innovations, 100 Million Jobs* (Pauli, 2010) and can be seen as a follow on from the Green Economy concept, in that it has the same desired outcome: increasing human well-being and social equity using available natural resources, whilst significantly reducing environmental risks and ecological scarcities.

The term was then taken up by representatives of SIDS and other coastal countries during the 2012 Rio Summit and has since seen widespread acceptance in development strategies and considerable academic and policy research.

The Blue Economy, however, is an evolving concept, and the dynamics of the ocean environment, population growth and political changes all impact on the ability to deliver the sustainable goals for this global resource. The idea of the oceans being a source of economic prosperity is nothing new of course and all nations with coastal borders have recognised the political and economic powers of their ocean territories.

It is the more recent realisation, however, of the environmental impact of this economic activity and the subsequent effect on the whole planet that has brought sustainable ocean practices into focus. SIDS are at the sharp end of this, with ocean jurisdictions that often far exceed their land areas, economies that have traditionally relied almost entirely on the oceans and a social and cultural structure that is closely aligned with the sea.

The growth of tourism in island states has significantly impacted the wealth of many of these nations but we have seen just how vulnerable that is to outside shocks and the impact that this can have on economies that have become heavily reliant on tourist income.

So whilst the Blue Economy has been and will continue to be essential to these small island states, this has to be balanced with the impact of global demographic trends and an increasing recognition of the importance of aligning future economic growth with maintaining or even restoring ocean health (Economist Intelligence Unit, 2015).

Even without increased exploitation of this resource, the oceans face rising degradation, depletion of fish stocks, habitat destruction, increased pollution, rising populations and climate change (Blasiak et al., 2019).

This is despite the 2015 Indian Ocean Rim Association (IORA) Ministerial Conference on the Blue Economy that saw the adoption of the Mauritius Declaration on the Blue Economy, putting in place the strategic goals for sustainable ocean resource management. It emphasised the importance of developing sustainable practices in fisheries and aquaculture, renewable ocean energy, seaport and shipping and the development of offshore hydrocarbon and mineral mining. It sets this declaration in the context of the United Nations' Sustainable Development Goals (SDGs) and particularly Goal 14 – the conservation and sustainable use of the oceans.

The issue of course with this declaration is the real possibility that, despite all the good intentions, a decoupling of increased activity in the four industry sectors noted earlier and environmental protection is a real possibility. For example, there are considerable concerns over the substantial environmental impact of seabed mining, the increased pollution from seaport development and increased shipping capacity, and the ability to deliver this growth in a sustainable manner. Indeed, Van Dover et al. (2017) argue that the scale of proposed seabed mining in particular is likely to cause inevitable and irreversible negative impacts on biodiversity.

This drive for increased exploitation and the requirements for sustainable development of these natural resources then call into question whether these two competing agendas really are reconcilable in practice. Arguments for the Blue Economy stress that these tensions are associated with its status as an 'alternative' model of growth, a shift from exploitative to sustainable economies.

When we look at the realities of the Blue Economy, rather than it being an alternative to traditional growth models, it sits very much within the recognised structures of economic development – that is, its growth is based on the exploitation of natural resources, tourism and physical goods exports.

However, the whole global economic model, the methods by which countries, communities and individual entrepreneurs create wealth, is shifting (World Trade Organisation, 2020). This is not a reworking of the narrative around the 'myth of continual growth', nor a plea to move to a rather utopian 'de-growth' agenda, but a recognition that there is a real shift in how value is created and commoditised and how the world's leading companies are increasingly digital- and knowledge-based.

So this is not a proposal to move economic growth away from the oceans as, for SIDS, the Blue Economy is central and essential but rather a suggestion that it cannot be seen as the only driver of socio-economic development. To do so would exclude not only the rise of the most dynamic global trade sector but also risks exacerbating the environmental impacts that Blue Economy strategies seek to ameliorate.

For example, one of the most threatened ocean ecosystems are coral reefs. Over the last three years, reefs around the world have suffered from mass coral bleaching due to a combination of marine pollution and global warming. It is estimated that 50% of the world's corals have been destroyed.

Yet coral reefs provide 500 million people with livelihoods through fishing and tourism and also contribute an estimated US$1 trillion to the global economy. Similarly, reefs are vital to help achieve the Aichi Biodiversity Targets and deliver the United Nations Sustainable Development Goals, especially 'life below water' (Gairin & Andrefouet, 2020).

The discussions on the Blue Economy come as a UN report on the effects of plastic pollution on coral reefs revealed that more than 800 marine and coastal species had had "some form of encounter with marine litter, of which the majority is plastic". They added that pollution increased the likelihood of coral disease, rising from 4% to 89% when corals were in contact with plastics. This, combined with over-fishing and increased infrastructure projects around these delicate environments, is increasing habitat degradation (United Nations Environment Programme, 2018).

For SIDS in particular, these coral regions are crucial to an overall healthy marine environment and the tourism sector. The growth of the Blue Economy and the resulting increase in activity around shipping, mining and fishing can only put more pressure on these regions that are already on a knife edge.

Whilst many will argue that by its definition, the notion of the Blue Economy is sustainable growth based on ocean resources, the reality is starting to look very different. It is that gap between the need to develop the ocean resource and the importance to that very resource of its environmental protection that makes SIDS vulnerable, not just to the usual economic and climactic shocks, but to the impact that a lack of innovation in thinking, research and business models will have.

If the goal is to deliver equitable and sustainable economic growth to coastal regions and SIDS, then the Blue Economy can only be a part of the solution. We have to take a multi-sector approach that recognises the paradigm shifts that have occurred in trade, wealth creation and economic growth and the huge opportunities that this shift opens up. Unless governments and key global bodies recognise this the outcome of economic growth based solely on the oceans will be the very loss of the resource it sought to sustainably develop and exploit.

The Blue Economy will be one of the most important areas for global economic inclusion and equality over the next decade but has to fulfil its whole remit – it has to be sustainable and environmentally positive. Statements and declarations have to translate into innovation and impact. This can only be achieved if the Blue Economy is seen as part of a whole and not the whole itself, and unfortunately at present, research and thinking are far too siloed.

The health of the oceans is perhaps the most pressing agenda of our time – just as important as climate change – and the suggestion that the Blue Economy, the marketisation and commoditisation of oceans resources, is the best way to protect them as well as provide economic growth for coastal communities seems flawed.

If no alternatives to the Blue Economy as a means for sustainable economic development for SIDS are explored, supported and invested in, then the pressure on ocean resources can only increase. In this case, the reality, however good the intentions are, will be very different from the theory and concept of Blue growth. This really is a simple case of risk reduction, because if all the eggs are in one basket, the potential for disaster is always there.

The dominance of tourism

Tourism generates significant amounts of income for SIDS but is hugely impactful in terms of pollution, is founded on a generally low-skill and low-paid local workforce and the majority of the profits do not stay in the regions in which they are generated.

Many SIDS rely heavily on tourism, thanks to their extraordinary natural landscapes, beaches, marine environments and cultural heritage. Tourism accounts for less than 5% of GDP in other developing countries but contributes over 20% for the majority of SIDS, with countries such as the Maldives economy seeing direct and indirect contributions from tourism amounting to 78% of GDP and 62% of employment (World Travel and Trade Council, 2018; International Monetary Fund, 2016). Tourism has been the main driver of many SIDS moving from low-income countries to middle- or upper-middle, but financial leakages from the sector often do not translate into positive impacts on the communities and individual livelihoods of island peoples.

There is often little 'spillover' from the tourist sector into the rest of the local economy with large quantities of food imports for the resorts and hotels, construction materials used in resort development and the repatriation of profits from tourist activity and land rents. So whilst the impact of tourism growth can be seen in GDP figures, this often does not translate into improved living standards for the local population as revenues brought into the region by foreign tourists flow back out again to foreign investors and holding companies (Bertram, 2016).

The risks stemming from over-reliance of SIDS on tourism became all too clear following the devastating impact of the 2020 Covid-19 pandemic on both lives and economies. The pandemic saw international tourism face its worst decline since records began with around 1.1 billion fewer people taking trips globally in 2020 (UNWTO, 2020).

Travel restrictions, the closure of airports and borders and the fears of travellers could see a decline in tourist arrivals if up to 80%, threatening the livelihoods of up to 120 million people and a loss of export revenues from tourism of over US$1 trillion (UNWTO, 2020).

For example, increasing the number of tourist beds in an already saturated geographical market will only increase biodiversity degradation, increase energy use and carbon footprint and more food and material waste produced. Some of that can certainly be ameliorated by implementing greater recycling, carbon reductions and habitat protection.

However, the reason behind tourism development is to create the much-needed jobs that support livelihoods and increase revenues and GDP. If some of that growth could be provided through other low-resource-intensive, high-skill and high-wage jobs, then the pressure to exploit the ocean is lessened.

Unfortunately, little has been written and espoused about the interconnectedness of other sectors, particularly digital, knowledge-based industries, to the success of Blue Economy implementation.

Cross-sector innovation and multi-sectoral strategic development are key here. The more isolated the emphasis is placed on the Blue Economy, the more focus, energy and research is conducted in this discipline without connection to other sectors, then the more pressure is placed upon it to achieve its goal of sustainable economic growth. And that is where it will fall down, because that pressure to deliver growth will override the sustainable aspect of the Blue Economy concept.

Development in SIDS regions then has to be approached as a holistic whole if we are to avoid the Blue Economy becoming unachievable, placing emphasis on digital, creative and knowledge-based economic drivers just as much as the ocean economy. We then have the possibility of not just maintaining but improving the health of the oceans, the most critical environment for the health of our planet and the one which is under the most extreme pressure.

Recognition of this fact and the actions needed to make it happen are well documented (Laffoley et al., 2019), as are the dire consequences of not taking significant and far-reaching action. Whist some research does look at the challenges of the Blue Economy and highlights some of the governance or implementation failings, they all fail to look beyond the boundaries of the Blue Economy to a wider and more integrated approach to the problem.

If there is a problem with over-exploitation of an ocean resource in a particular region, then we can certainly examine how that resource can be accessed more sustainably, but we can also look at how every other sector in that regional economy can support that resource, to help drive innovative solutions and to allow for a less intense exploitation.

A case study of the Maldives

The Maldives has, to a large extent, achieved its economic success of the last 40 years by developing its many islands into high-end tourist resorts. Strong growth in the tourism sector, with support from fisheries and tourism-related activities, enabled the Maldives to transition from least-developed to middle-income status by 2011. In spite of a number of adverse internal and external factors, its growth performance has been strong, with GDP per capita rising from $200 in 1978 to $11,890 in 2018 (Asian Development Bank, 2019), the highest in South Asia.

This record provides inspiring lessons for other small island economies. Yet the country continues to face great challenges in making growth more socially inclusive and regionally balanced. Economic disparities have widened between

Malé and the other islands and between groups of different socio-economic status. The wide dispersion of the population, coupled with transport infrastructure challenges, hampers the creation of sizeable domestic markets and presents a formidable challenge in sustaining growth and providing adequate public services.

These inadequacies in maritime transport coupled with limited availability of domestic skilled labour have held back private sector investment outside high-end tourism, yet this need not be the case if support for more knowledge-based, digital-creative sectors can be supported and invested in.

To do this though, post-secondary educational attainment has to be increased, particularly outside the capital, as this leaves the national labour force with a lack of skills and forces a heavy reliance on expatriate labour. It also sees the Maldives with a relatively high youth unemployment level at 15.3% and despite its position as a middle-income country, levels of poverty, particularly in the southern atolls, remain at around 1 in 5 (World Bank, 2020c).

Overcoming this will require substantial investment, which, given the impacts of Covid-19, is currently constrained by the limited budgetary room and the increasing public sector debt burden. Creating more inclusive growth focused around a higher-skill, knowledge-based economy will also require a sharper focus on the development of entrepreneurship and the expansion of micro, small and medium enterprises (MSMEs), which are an important source of productive employment. Currently, however, access to credit is weak and its cost high, with smaller firms having particular difficulty in getting long-term credit (World Bank, 2019).

At the same time, the country's small size and dispersion create enormous challenges in terms of public service delivery. The previous government had sought to tackle this through consolidation – to create scale in economic activities and efficiency in delivering various services by migrating the population into fewer islands. However, the issues around population congestion in Malé are now severe (Asfa, 2020; Rasheed & Zakariyya, 2017).

The Maldives' growth performance has been highly successful considering these internal and external challenges, but the importance of tourism has also exposed the economy to greater volatility, as we have seen recently.

External developments such as the Asian Financial Crisis of 1997–1998, the Indian Ocean tsunami of 2004 and the 2007–2008 global financial crisis demonstrated how the Maldives' heavy dependence on one sector – tourism – creates underlying vulnerabilities. These past shocks have been overwhelmed by the collapse of tourism during the global Covid-19 shutdown in the first quarter of 2020.

Tourism, as the major source of foreign exchange revenue, will continue to be a mainstay of the Maldivian economy however, despite the impacts of the Covid-19 pandemic. The year 2019 proved to be one of the most successful years ever for the industry, welcoming more than 1.7 million tourists – a 14.7% increase on the previous year (Travel Trade Maldives, 2020), and despite the dramatic collapse in tourist arrivals in 2020, a slow and steady recovery is expected (World Bank, 2020b).

The impacts of Covid-19 and economic uncertainty

That recovery however is extremely uncertain given the possible ongoing and extended impacts of Covid-19 on regional and global economic uncertainty.

The Asian Development Bank's March 2020 Report (ADB, 2020) singled out the Maldives as being the country in Asia worst affected by the lost tourism, with an 11.3% drop in GDP growth rate for 2020. Although the bank then predicts a 13.7% growth bounceback in 2021, that figure is unpredictable given the volatile nature of the global economy.

The knock-on effect of this of course will see the Maldives hard-pressed to service its international debts. A large proportion of this was accumulated under the previous administration and is now proving to be a significant downward pressure on the Maldives' ability to recover from the recent pandemic. Loans totalling $1.4 from China were used to fund an infrastructure building programme tied to the superpower's multibillion dollar Belt and Road Initiative. The projects included a bridge linking Malé, the capital, to the main airport on an adjacent island. The repayments of that loan and the subsequent pressure from China to 'pay up' again put further pressure on an already beleaguered economy.

The World Bank also highlighted that because of these pressures the national poverty rate was expected to increase as households already close to the poverty line would fall below it due to the loss of tourism-related income sources (World Bank, 2020a, Country Overview). US credit rating agency Fitch downgraded the Maldives to "B" and revised its outlook from stable to negative.

A positive outlook for the Maldives

Despite all these challenges, the Maldives has a strong and well-established brand in its tourism sector, and the bounceback for 2021 could be strong. It can also look to some key areas of development outside its core Blue Economy strengths.

The start-up community is beginning to develop with input and support from local companies as well as established international organisations such as Techstars. The Startup Maldives Network (SMN) was initiated by local company Sparkhub and aims to develop the entrepreneurship ecosystem in the Maldives and become a hub for the region.

Investment into such networks, from both a structural and an individual start-up level is going to be essential if the economic diversification that has taken such a central place in SIDS thinking is to be realised. Along with this, the development of expert, focused accelerators, with an emphasis on digital-creative and knowledge-based sectors and allied to clear runways, must be a priority for both the government and the international finance community.

The launch of 5G networks in the Maldives by local telecom companies Dhiraagu and Ooredoo is another very positive step along this road and offers businesses and entrepreneurs greater access and opportunity in the streaming and e-commerce sectors.

These two important elements should give investors, both institutional and individual, cause to look at the Maldives as an opportunity to invest and support young creative and technology-driven companies with real potential. The recovery from Covid-19 and the resultant global recession for Maldivians must be driven by such developments, where the valuable human resource of the country is not overlooked for the more usual natural resource of the oceans. The two really can support and innovate each other.

Increasing global economic uncertainty

The example of the Maldives is a microcosm of the challenges and opportunities now faced by island states. With the global economic system facing greater uncertainty, pressure and upheaval than at any time in the last 100 years, the impact of these forces on sustainable development in SIDS will only increase.

This dynamic uncertainty means that small island states have to innovate in their thinking around inclusive and sustainable growth, the sectors in which they invest, and the policy and strategic frameworks that their governments put in place.

This is why the digital-creative-knowledge economy will be so important to these regions. The vulnerabilities previously discussed will come into sharp focus with the economic uncertainty that is now all too present.

Alongside that however, there is now a feeling that low-carbon economies, markets and technologies, coupled with a growing move in global trade towards digital, creative and knowledge-based products, actually make good financial sense for the private sector.

To address these complex challenges, there is a need to accelerate the transformation of the entire economic system, driven by climate need, the engines of the Fourth Industrial Revolution and a much greater understanding of – and implementation of – the opportunities and strengths of a creative, knowledge-based economy.

The final point still has some way to go in terms of acceptance and understanding by governments and key international groups, with 'creative industries' still being seen simply as arts and cultural heritage and often consigned to footnotes or single-line entries at the end of economic development strategies.

This is despite the numerous conferences, strategies, white papers and forums happening around the world on the benefits of the creative economy. There is almost a neo-colonial attitude around the creative industries and the ability of SIDS to build sustainable creative economies, harking back to the scholars of the 1960s and their presumption of the economic non-viability that surrounded that period's wave of island state sovereignty (Briguglio, 2014).

The research and work around the sustainability of SIDS is a prime example of this. Despite virtually unanimous agreement on the need to broaden island economies to ameliorate the impacts of climate and economic shocks, vulnerability is still discussed in terms of distance from markets, economies of scale and lack of natural resource beyond the oceans.

Whilst some authors have sought to balance this narrative of vulnerability with one of resilience (Briguglio & Cordina, 2004), the development strategies proposed for this resilience still fall very much into the traditional sector architecture – heritage crafts, financial services, specialist foods, and so on.

An example of how this is translated into strategic thinking can be seen in the Third International Conference on SIDS back in 2014 that generated an outcome document known as the SIDS Accelerated Modalities of Action (SAMOA) Pathway adopted by the General Assembly of the United Nations later that same year. The SAMOA Pathway set out a five-point action plan to support SIDS in their efforts to achieve sustainable development.

These were:

1   Enhancing island capacities to achieve sustainable development through education and the reinforcement of human and institutional capacities.
2   Enhancing SIDS' resilience and the sustainability of human interactions with ecological, freshwater and ocean systems.
3   Supporting SIDS in the management of social transformations and the promotion of social inclusion and social justice.
4   Preserving tangible and intangible cultural heritage and promoting the culture for island sustainable development.
5   Increasing connectivity, information management and knowledge sharing.

This pathway document called upon the international community to support SIDS in designing and implementing their own innovative cultural policies to strengthen heritage and creativity and leverage the economic, social and natural benefits of culture. The 'creative industries' were mentioned in that section, but it is revealing to see how it is contextualised and aligned. The document highlights preserving tangible and intangible cultural heritage and promoting culture for island sustainable development, which is certainly important, but again there is a failure to understand that creative industries as a tool for sustainable development is far wider than cultural heritage.

Computer games design and production, film and television production, digital design, visual effects and immersive technology are the key drivers of the explosion of creative industries as a global economic force. If SIDS are to exploit these sectors then the there has to be a recognition that cultural heritage is not the creative industries, it is simply a small part. The majority of impacts that the creative industries have had on the global economic and trade systems has come because of its transformation through digital technology.

So whilst the objectives in the document recognise that creative industries are crucial to the economic and social well-being of SIDS, it is the lack of connecting this to the opportunities of technology that has held it back, and continues to do so.

The need for research innovation

The evaluation above is still persisting despite radical changes in how economies can diversify, how populations can connect and how new skills can drive growth.

In the vast majority of reports and academic discussions around the vulnerabilities of SIDS, the above arguments as to why the diversification and resilience is difficult to achieve are all-pervasive. Little, if any, work has been done around the impact of the Fourth Industrial Revolution or the opportunities of digital exports as a driver of sustainable development in small island developing states. This is a serious oversight, not just in academic arguments but more importantly in the real world of policy, strategy and investment. We can see from this then that one of the most concerning vulnerabilities for SIDS is the lack of innovative thinking about how these regions can grow sustainably.

Whilst climate change, clean energy and the Blue Economy are of course central to the economic and social success of SIDS, failing to recognise the impact and importance of other factors, particularly digital, creative and knowledge-based innovation economies, can, as we have seen, undermine the work and investment in the more traditional Blue Economy sectors. Indeed, if these areas are not addressed, then the ability of SIDS to overcome the other vulnerabilities is severely impaired.

An example of this is the perception of natural resources. The small land mass of these island states is a significant limiter on agriculture, manufacturing and industry, yet there is little discussion in the hundreds of reports and academic papers on SIDS on the value of their human resource as a driver of innovation-led and knowledge-based GDP and economic growth.

It is as if the human population of SIDS can only be seen as a part of existing traditional industries. If we look however at the countries of the Global North, the narrative is very different. Here, innovation, entrepreneurship, the knowledge economy and creative skills are seen as the most important aspects of human resource development for the twenty-first century, as economies respond to the challenges of new technologies and new industry sectors.

The spread of these new technologies has given young entrepreneurs, almost regardless of their location and access to natural resource, the ability to build products that have market value, have global reach and can be effectively monetised through digital distribution channels. For the population of SIDS that have always been seen as isolated from global markets, this has the potential for a game-changing shift.

The importance of this paradigm shift for island states and small communities is noticeably lacking though on the part of researchers, NGOs and governments. This lack of innovative thinking presents a serious external pressure on the ability of these island states to crucially become more self-reliant and resilient and therefore to take the lead in driving their own sustainable growth.

We have seen many discussions and statements on the need to 'build back better' following the Covid-19 pandemic and the global recession. Innovation, in all its forms, will be central to that rebuild, but innovation is not just about doing things differently; it is about doing different things. This is the challenge we have in putting this innovation into practice, not just for small island states to build their resilience and economic potential but to deliver the whole SDG agenda over the next decade.

A key part of that challenge will be producing high-quality, applied and relevant research that can then inform the strategies and practices for that delivery. Whilst there is some outstanding research being conducted around SIDS, the
focus is narrow and could be seen to exclude important investigations into more
innovative approaches to these island economies.

Figure 1.1 shows a breakdown of a total of 129,000 papers published since
2016 listed on Google Scholar that include Small Island Developing States in
their title. Papers were then classified into groups around climate change, tourism,
the Blue Economy and others.

What is clear from the graph is the lack of breadth in research subjects for small
island states.

Whilst the breakdown of academic publishing may not seem important outside
the Academy, the fact is that this research then goes on to inform the majority
of policy interventions and the strategic thinking of individual governments and
global organisations.

This lack of diversity then has serious impacts on how these island states
can develop, grow and be part of the new digital global economy. It increases
the vulnerability of SIDS through the lack of innovative thinking and applied
research.

An example of how this narrow research focus can impact the real world can be
seen in the 2014 UN Conference on Small Island Developing States. It identified
six clusters of priority areas that the Partnership Dialogues for SIDS looked to
address respectively to advance the sustainable development of SIDS.

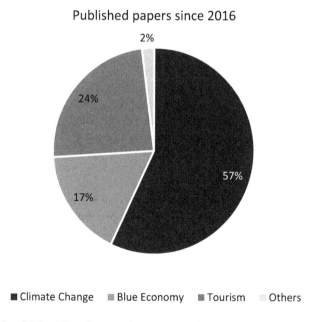

Published papers since 2016

Figure 1.1 Small Island Development States Research Papers.

These were:

1 Sustainable economic development
2 Climate change and disaster risk management
3 Social development in SIDS
4 Health and non-communicable diseases (NCDs), youth and women
5 Sustainable energy; oceans, seas and biodiversity
6 Water and sanitation, food security and waste management.

Now these are obviously broad strategic areas, but across all of them and noticeable by their absence was any mention of digital entrepreneurship, creative industries or knowledge economy development. This is indicative of the wider approach to development and resilience in these regions. It was only later, in suggested partnership developments, that entrepreneurship and creative industries were mentioned.

This lack is however not restricted to discussions of SIDS. The creative industries as a whole, despite being the fastest growing global sector with a value in excess of $2.5 trillion, still lag behind more traditional industry sectors in governments' and international organisations' actions. This is despite the many strategy documents, white papers and reports published around the impact and importance of the creative economy. For developing regions and SIDS, the value of digital-creative growth is virtually invisible. When it is discussed, it is framed in the culture and heritage argument.

If the technological revolution of the twenty-first century is, as is so often said, going to change everything, then, as a consequence, everything has to change. Unfortunately, the current approach to delivering an innovative sustainable development strategy for these island regions is bound by somewhat traditional thinking. This research focus, however, is in some ways understandable as climate change and environmental degradation are the key challenges of our time. The Blue Economy is the key sector for many SIDS. However, these challenges are not going to be met through this narrow research focus.

The environmental and economic vulnerabilities of SIDS will not be addressed and overcome without innovation and creative thinking in terms of both the specific challenges themselves and in how we approach the whole process of research and application. A lot of research discusses the vulnerability of SIDS due to their geographical isolation from major markets and trade hubs, their increased transportation costs and the difficulties of developing their human resources.

Whilst this may have been true in the last decade, the global economy is changing so rapidly that the rise of digital exports and of highly connected communities and the spread of fast broadband means that this isolation is rapidly losing its importance. This has to be reflected in the research and the understanding of how SIDS can develop economically, socially and environmentally

A key limitation for understanding economic development in SIDS, particularly around digital-creative economies, is the lack of data. This can mean that databases are completed with approximations based on assumptions, and alternative assumptions could have produced different approximations (Briguglio, 2016).

Whilst, as we have seen, there is extensive literature on climate change, the Blue Economy and ocean environments in relation to SIDS, the areas of knowledge economies, innovation and digital-creative entrepreneurship remain significantly under-researched, resulting in a lack of high-quality and up-to-date data on these crucial aspects of SIDS development.

Routes to resilience for SIDS economies

So the narrative of vulnerability, whilst undoubtedly based on solid evidence, must not become all-pervasive and must be countered by the same sectors, innovations and advances that are powering the developed world.

The weight of literature around climate impacts, ocean degradation, overtourism and the need for heavy investment to offset these effects overlook the importance of innovation, human resource development and trade in other sectors. It also underestimates the potential for developing knowledge-based, creative local economies that, thanks to the impact of the rapidly advancing technologies of production and distribution, allow these traditionally isolated regions to insert themselves into the new global trade opportunities.

Resilience therefore for SIDS is not just a case of science and technology mitigating the effects of climate change or developing new clean energy sources but of framing sustainable development for these regions as encompassing all aspects of economy, society, culture, innovation and government. It is revealing just how little focus is placed on developing the other great resource of island nations – its people.

The development of island entrepreneurship by island peoples is discussed in later chapters, but whilst the challenges of limited land area and domestic markets, finite resources, physical isolation from global markets and increased transport costs are all correct, citing them as the reason for low levels of entrepreneurship is reductionist and no longer entirely holds true. More important today are the reducing flows of FDI, restricted research capability, the implementation of favourable local finance terms for MSMEs and building a sufficiently skilled human resource.

So resilience in all its forms is multifaceted, involving economic, environmental, political and social factors (Briguglio, 2014), and needs to be a key part of the strategic approach to sustainable development, not only working across all these areas but also developing strong education, skills, entrepreneurship and innovation frameworks. In looking at resilience and sustainable economic development, long-term and successfully implementable solutions can only come from the islands themselves. Support and investment from the international community is essential, but in the past this has taken on an unbalanced approach, with projects and initiatives, however well meaning, far too often being 'done to' rather than 'done with' the islands and its peoples.

Broadening SIDS economies

If true resilience for SIDS is to be achieved, then first and foremost must be the broadening of their economic bases. The reasons for narrow economies in SIDS are well documented, with tourism and fisheries dominating many economies to an almost exclusive extent. The importance of these sectors then inevitably draws the majority of research, funding, policy and strategy development and international discussion.

It is revealing to see the language used in these research and policy documents, arguing that due to their extensive marine areas, the future resource base for such countries is marine. In the traditional sense of course this is entirely correct, but one rarely sees human resources discussed in relation to the economic development of SIDS.

Some SIDS economies do still have natural resources/commodity exploitations as important parts of their economies, such as Trinidad and Tobago with petroleum, natural gas and asphalt, and Papua New Guinea with timber and coffee production along with gold, silver and copper mining. Sustainability of these natural resources of course is a significant limiting factor here. The drive to global decarbonisation brings into question many natural resource–centred industries, and it is essential to see how these traditional extractive industries can be replaced in the coming years.

Sustained and inclusive economic growth in SIDS also requires the strengthening of capacity-building and investment in infrastructure development and job creation, particularly in the area of ICT and financial services. Investment in human capital must be complemented by productive investment in the real economy to create employment opportunities and by inclusive financial systems that are accessible for marginalised groups, including youth, women, indigenous peoples and local communities.

Addressing youth unemployment could potentially help ease many social problems such as high levels of petty crime and violence in several countries. We have already seen the high employment value that creative and digital industries have for youth employment, so developing these sectors offers a dynamic way forward for island governments to address youth issues. These sectors also help engage an often educationally disengaged youth, certainly post-secondary, so educational aspiration and attainment can also be a key factor in addressing the problems of youth unemployment.

Many SIDS are also challenged by underemployment in rural areas as well as high urban unemployment. The two, combined with inadequate economic growth, have contributed to large-scale emigration of skilled labour, otherwise known as 'brain drain'.

Resilience then for SIDS can only be achieved through a multi-functional and multi-sector approach that looks beyond the norms of existing economic sectors, development practices and international interventions.

Conclusion

The following chapters set out a roadmap for how this can be achieved, from reimaging the relationship of industry, government and academia, commonly referred to as the Triple Helix, to building digital-creative ecosystems, supporting creative entrepreneurship and looking at concrete methods for supporting and orchestrating that delicate ecosystem.

For the Blue Economy to work, if it is to be in any way deliverable in the real world for small island states, then it has to be actively supported by other sectors. In the face of worsening ocean degradation, biodiversity loss, rising populations and challenging global economics, SIDS need the international development, academic and financial communities to remove their blinkers, recognise their past and present mistakes and look beyond the panacea of the Blue Economy.

Only then can these islands secure their economic, social and cultural futures.

References

Alonso Rodriguez, J., Cortez, A.L. & Klasen, S. 2014. LDC and Other Country Groupings: How Useful Are Current Approaches to Classify Countries in a More Heterogeneous Developing World? CDP Background Papers, United Nations, Department Economics and Social Affairs.

Asfa, S.A. 2020. Economic Development of the Maldives Islands. *Politics, Economy and Innovation*, 1(30).

Asian Development Bank. 2019. *Maldives: Economic Update 2019*. Asian Development Bank, Philippines.

Asian Development Bank, 2020. *Multihazard Risk Atlas of Maldives*. Asian Development Bank, Manila, Philippines.

Bartelme, D., Costinot, A., Donaldson, D. & Rodriguez-Clare, A. 2018. External Economies of Scale and Industrial Policy: A View from Trade. Working paper.

Bertram, G. 2016. *Implications of the Cook Islands Graduation from Development Assistance Committee (DAC) Eligibility*. Ministry of Finance and Economic Management, Government of the Cook Islands, Cook Islands.

Blasiak, R., Wabnitz, C.C., Daw, T., Berger, M., Blandon, A., Carneiro, G., Crona, B., Davidson, M.F., Guggisberg, S., Hills, J. & Mallin, F. 2019. Towards Greater Transparency in Funding for Sustainable Marine Fisheries and Healthy Oceans. *Marine Policy*, 107, p. 103508.

Briguglio, L. 2014. A Vulnerability and Resilience Framework for Small States. In Bynoe-Lewis, D. (Ed.), *Building the Resilience of Small States: A Revised Framework*, pp. 1–102. Commonwealth Secretariat, London.

Briguglio, L. 2016. Exposure to External Shocks and Economic Resilience of Countries: Evidence from Global Indicators. *Journal of Economic Studies,* 43(6), pp. 1057–1078.

Briguglio, L. & Cordina, G. 2004. Malta's Competitiveness Standing and the EU Lisbon Agenda. In Briguglio, L. & Cordina, G. (Eds.), *Competitiveness Strategies for Small States*, pp. 58–74. Formatek Publishing, Blata I-Bajda.

Briguglio, L., Cordina, G., Farrugia, N. & Vella, S. 2009. Economic Vulnerability and Resilience: Concepts and Measurements. *Oxford Development Studies*, 37(3), pp. 229–247.

Colgan, C. 2018. Climate Change and the Blue Economy of the Indian Ocean. In Attri, V.N. & Bohler-Mulleris, N. (Eds.), *The Blue Economy Handbook of the Indian Ocean*. Africa Institute of South Africa, Pretoria.

De la Croix, D., Docquier, F. & Schiff, M. 2014. Brain Drain and Economic Performance in Small Island Developing States. In *The Socio-Economic Impact of Migration Flows*. Springer International Publishing, New York.

Economist Intelligence Unit. 2015. The Blue Economy; Growth, Opportunity and a Sustainable Ocean Economy. Briefing paper for the World Ocean Summit, 2015, London.

Gairin, E. & Andrefouet, S. 2020. Role of Habitat Definition on Aichi Target 11: Examples from New Caledonian Coral Reefs. *Marine Policy*, 116, June, p. 103951.

International Monetary Fund, 2016. *Maldives Debt Sustainability Analysis*. International Monetary Fund, Washington, DC.

Laffoley, D., Baxter, J.M., Amon, D.J., et al. 2019. Eight Urgent, Fundamental and Simultaneous Steps Needed to Restore Ocean Health and the Consequences for Humanity and the Planet of Inaction or Delay. *Aquatic Conservation*, 30, pp. 194–208.

McDermott, A. 2016. Coral Bleaching Event Is Longest on Record. *Science News*.

Organisation for Economic Cooperation and Development. 2018a. *Creditor Reporting System Database*. OECD, Paris.

Organisation for Economic Cooperation and Development. 2018b. *Financing for Development in Small Island Developing States: A Focus on Concessional Finance*. OECD, Paris.

Organisation for Economic Cooperation and Development. 2018c. *Making Development Co-operation Work for Small Island Developing States*. OECD, Paris.

Pauli, G. 2010. *The Blue Economy: 10 Years, 100 Innovations, 100 Million Jobs*. Paradigm Publications, Brookline, MA.

Ponte, A.D., Delton, A.W., Kline, R. & Seltzer, N.A. 2017. Passing it Along: Experiments on Creating the Negative Externalities of Climate Change. *The Journal of Politics*, 79(4), pp. 1444–1448.

Quak, E. 2019. *How Losing Access to Concessional Finance Affects Small Island Developing States*. K4 helpdesk Report No 626. Institute of Development Studies, Brighton, UK.

Rasheed, R. & Zakariyya, N. 2017. Small, Dispersed, Sustainable and Prosperous: An Alternative Paradigm to Population Consolidation in the Maldives. *The Solutions Journal*, 8.

Travel Trade Maldives. 2020. *Maldives Tourism Industry Forecast 2023*. Travel Trade Maldives, Male, Maldives.

United Nations Environment Programme. 2018. *Single Use Plastics: A Roadmap for Sustainability*. UNEP, New York.

United Nations Office of the High Representative for the Least Developed Countries, Landlocked Countries and Small Island Developing States. 2015. *Small Island Developing States in Numbers, Climate Change Edition 2015*. United Nations, New York.

United Nations World Tourism Organisation. 2020. Impact Assessment of the COVID-19 Outbreak on International Tourism. Accessed at www.UNWTO.org.

Van Dover, C.L., Ardron, J.A., Escobar, E., Gianni, M., Gjerde, K.M., Jaeckel, A., et al. 2017. Biodiversity Loss from Deep Sea Mining. *Nature Geoscience*, 10, pp. 464–465.

World Bank. 2016. *Small States Forum 2016 – Towards a Resilient and Equitable Future; Opportunities for Financing and Partnerships*. World Bank, Washington, DC.

World Bank. 2018. *Comoros Poverty Assessment*. World Bank, Washington, DC.

World Bank. 2020a. Country Profile. Accessed at http://worldbank.org/en/country/Maldives

World Bank. 2020b. Maldives Development Update. In *Stormy Seas*. World Bank, Washington, DC.

World Bank. 2020c. Maldives Overview 2020. Accessed at http://worldbank.org/en/country/Maldives.

World Bank/IMF. 2019. *Joint World Bank-IMF Debt Sustainability Analysis 2019*. World Bank, Washington, DC. Accessed at http://hdl.handle.net/10986/32580.

World Trade Organisation, Annual Report. 2020. WTO.

World Travel and Trade Council. 2018. *Travel and Tourism Global Economic Impact and Issues, 2018*. WTTC, London.

Yamamoto, L. & Esteban, M. 2014. Climate Change and its Effects on Atoll Island States. In *Atoll Island States and International Law*, pp. 35–103. Springer, Berlin.

2 The Sustainable Development Goals and the digital-creative economy

Introduction

The Industrial Revolution 4.0 will open up new avenues for science-driven creativity and innovation. The world must resort to the ultimate renewable resource: human ingenuity and creativity. Creativity is at the heart of sustainability, rooted in sustainable social, economic, environmental and cultural practices.

(D'Orville, H. 2019)

The breadth, scope and ambition of the United Nations' Sustainable Development Goals (SDGs) are both inspiring and truly daunting. A vision for what the world could be, they are a mix of social, economic and cultural targets that are, despite the huge challenges, galvanising partners to come together and act.

The cultural and creative industries are discussed in terms of both their global economic value and their non-monetary value, as both a source of jobs and revenue and a driver of social inclusion, dialogue and understanding.

What is often missing is the step taken beyond these broad statements and declarations into action and implementation and a recognition of where the value of the creative and cultural industries (CCI) really lies for the SDGs.

One can find pledges such as the Creative Industries Pact for Sustainable Action, an international initiative to bring the film and television industries in line with a set of actions to support the Paris Agreement on climate change. This is no doubt a positive move, with around 70 organisations now signed up, but the real importance of the creative and cultural sectors to the SDGs lies not in the rather CSR-style nod to sustainable action by companies in the developed world but in the opportunities these sectors open up for new avenues of sustainable growth in regions of the Global South, such as with SIDS.

For SIDS, the SDGs are central to their prosperity, security and social and cultural coherence. In this, the 'decade of delivery' for these goals, it is essential to look beyond the traditional approaches and innovation methods if we are to make these islands and communities safe, prosperous and sustainable.

Making this happen though will require a change in the approach to achieving the SDGs in island states and the relationship to the implementation of goals by national governments and the international development and research community. In particular, this is about seeing the SDGs as a strategy that needs a sectorally integrated approach, a cross-sector and multi-sector industry partnership that puts digital-creative innovation at its heart.

The origin of the goals

Understanding the nature of the SDGs and their origins can help in how we change the way that they are conceptualised and implemented. Sustainable development itself has been defined in numerous ways, but the most frequently quoted definition is from the World Commission on Environment and Development report entitled *Our Common Future*, also known as the Brundtland Report:

> Sustainable development is development that meets the needs of the present without compromising the ability of future generations to meet their own needs.
> (World Commission on Environment and Development, 1987)

Although the start of the sustainable development concept is widely recognised as originating at the 1972 UN Conference on the Human Environment, one could argue that it actually began a decade earlier with the publication of Rachel Carson's book *Silent Spring* (Carson, 1962). This book highlighted the dangers of industrial pollution and pesticides on the natural environment and sparked a greater societal awareness of the costs to the natural world of unchecked industrial activity. This was given further weight by the US Government's National Environmental Policy Act of 1969, which was enacted in response to the devastating environmental impact of the Santa Barbara oil spill that same year.

The first 'modern' use of the term 'sustainable' in its relation to economic growth came in the Club of Rome report, *Limits to Growth*, published in March 1972. Written by a group of scientists led by MIT's Dennis and Donella Meadows, the report described the goal of a "state of global equilibrium" as being 'sustainable' (Meadows et al., 1972). Twenty years later, and 30 years after Carson's seminal book, the 1992 United Nations Conference on Environment and Development (UNCED), also known as the 'Earth Summit', gave significant international impetus and weight to the consensus that economic development had to be balanced by environmental protection and greater social inclusion. The Agenda 21 adoption at that conference emphasised the critical nature of environmental protection and that

> integration of environment and development concerns and greater attention to them will lead to the fulfilment of basic needs, improved living standards for all, better protected and managed ecosystems and a safer, more prosperous future. No nation can achieve this on its own; but together we can – in a global partnership for sustainable development.
> (United Nations Conference on Environment and Development, 1992)

In 2012, 20 years on from the 'Earth Summit', the UN Conference on Sustainable Development became known as the 'Rio+20' conference and shows the gradual movement of the international community towards a more systematic collaboration on the key environmental, economic, social and cultural challenges that the world faces.

The creation of the 17 SDGs as we know them today happened at the UN General Assembly in 2015, where these 17 goals were broken down into 169 targets aimed at bringing together economic and social development with environmental and cultural protection (Figure 2.1).

Goal 1	**No Poverty**	**End poverty in all its forms everywhere**
Goal 2	**Zero Hunger**	**End hunger, achieve food security and improved nutrition and promote sustainable agriculture**
Goal 3	**Good Health and Wellbeing**	**Ensure healthy lives and promote wellbeing for all at all ages**
Goal 4	**Quality Education**	**Ensure inclusive and equitable quality education and promote lifelong learning opportunities for all**
Goal 5	**Gender Equality**	**Achieve gender equality and empower all women and girls**
Goal 6	**Clean Water & Sanitation**	**Ensure availability and sustainable management of water and sanitation for all**
Goal 7	**Affordable & Clean Energy**	**Ensure access to affordable, reliable, sustainable and modern energy for all**
Goal 8	**Decent Work & Economic Growth**	**Promote sustained, inclusive and sustainable economic growth, full and productive employment and decent work for all**
Goal 9	**Industry, Innovation & Infrastructure**	**Build resilient infrastructure, promote inclusive and sustainable industrialisation and foster innovation**
Goal 10	**Reduced Inequalities**	**Reduce inequalities within and between countries**
Goal 11	**Sustainable Cities & Communities**	**Make cities and human settlements inclusive, safe, resilient and sustainable**
Goal 12	**Responsible Consumption & Production**	**Ensure sustainable consumption and production patters**
Goal 13	**Climate Action**	**Take urgent action to combat climate change and its impacts**
Goal 14	**Life Below Water**	**Conserve and sustainable use the oceans, seas and marine resources for sustainable development**
Goal 15	**Life on Land**	**Protect, restore and promote sustainable use of terrestrial ecosystems, sustainably manage forests, combat desertification, halt and reverse land degradation and halt biodiversity loss**
Goal 16	**Peace, Justice & Strong Institutions**	**Promote peaceful and inclusive societies for sustainable development, provide access to justice for all and build effective, accountable and inclusive institutions at all levels.**
Goal 17	**Partnerships for the Goals**	**Strengthen the means of implementation and revitalise the global partnership for sustainable development**

Figure 2.1 The United Nations Sustainable Development Goals

These SDGs have been set as a mechanism to drive global cooperative action, with their implementation seen as primarily being the responsibility of individual countries. That implementation strategy however relies on the concerted and cooperative action of these national governments, and it is the tension between international targets, national strategies and national or even sub-national priorities that has seen progress towards these goals being slow and limited. Whilst some goals have seen progress, such as improving maternal and child health, better women's representation in government and some progress on access to utilities such as electricity, others have actually gone backwards, namely increased levels of poverty, growing food insecurity and the deterioration of natural environments, particularly the oceans.

In the face of the Covid-19 pandemic, that progress has taken a further substantial hit. The UN Annual Sustainable Development Goals Report for 2020 makes for grim reading (UN, 2020), highlighting that an estimated 71 million people will be pushed back into extreme poverty in 2020, the first rise in global poverty since 1998. Ocean acidification is accelerating, land degradation continues and biodiversity loss is at a greater risk than ever before.

This is on top of the increase in underemployment and unemployment, the unequal impact of the pandemic on the poorest citizens and countries, and the loss of education for young people globally. Inevitably then, resources available to countries to progress the SDGs will be severely hit as nations try to offset the economic impacts of the health emergency.

So despite all research, international conferences and forums and high-level commitments that governments had made, action, implementation and progress on the ground have fallen significantly behind.

Much has been talked about in terms of creating a 'new normal' and of 'building back better'. That has to apply to how we now approach the next ten years of action towards achieving the 2030 Agenda. Repeating the actions of the last five years as a way forward for reaching the SDGs simply won't work. If those failures of strategy and implementation were not clear before Covid-19, then they certainly are now. Central to this is not expecting individual governments to implement strategies and actions in isolation in the hope that this can, in some ad hoc way, get us over the line.

Reconceptualising partnerships for the 2030 Agenda

The final SDG is key to successfully implementing and achieving the preceding 16 specific goals and the whole 2030 Agenda. 'Partnerships for the Goals' are focused on building the mechanisms of implementation through the collaborative action of partnerships. These partnerships though need to be more than just the usual intergovernmental forums with aid organisations and international agencies. It needs a disruptive approach that seeds new thinking and new partnerships, bringing education, industry, disparate sectors, creators and entrepreneurs together to deliver the new thinking that is so desperately needed.

The discussion has to broaden out from the dialogues created by the usual leaders around the oceans economy, cultural heritage, tourism and the environment. If SIDS are to benefit from the delivery of the SDGs, then the new powerhouse of the global economy must be front and centre. A strong indigenous digital-creative economy has the power to deliver innovation and sustainable growth across every other sector.

The ability to create strong, focused, accountable and properly resourced partnerships will be at the heart of delivering the 2030 Agenda – whether that is the largely government-led Global Partnership for Sustainable Development, aimed at facilitating cross-border cooperation, or the variances of global, national, subnational or city level, multi-stakeholder partnerships.

The terms of how these partnerships are structured will vary greatly, but the main focus will be on sharing expertise and resources in supporting the implementation of the goals (United Nations, 2015). The UN resolution on enhancing partnership cooperation adopted at the General Assembly in December 2018 (United Nations, 2018) outlines the importance of public, private and civic partners in delivering the 2030 Agenda but does not set out any particular frameworks for these partnerships beyond a broad definition as "collaborative relations".

Dodds (2015) highlights the importance of establishing more decentralised and participatory approaches to this collaboration, described as Type II partnerships. These are generally focused around a specific goal and include national and subnational governments, the private sector and civil society. These partnerships have been especially noticeable in the approach to SDG delivery in SIDS.

The Third International Conference on Small Island Developing States in 2014 saw nearly 300 partnerships register for the conference, with a current total of more than 500, aimed at addressing key areas such as sustainable energy, seas and biodiversity and youth and women. An outcome of the conference was the establishment of the partnership framework to ensure proper delivery, monitoring and implementation. The majority of these partnerships are led by UN organisations, with IGOs, NGOs and civil society partnerships leading a minority share.

Whilst this partnership framework and the outcomes of the partnerships are generally positive, monitoring, review and reporting are uneven in terms of both quality and timescales. Out of the 541 currently registered partnerships, 356 partnerships are two years or more overdue or noted as inactive (United Nations Small Island Developing States Action Platform, 2020). This is obviously a concern, and it is important to investigate and understand the reasons behind this in order to implement better support for and management of these partnerships. The partnerships framework, properly supported, managed and monitored, can be a powerful tool for SIDS to make significant progress on implementing the SDGs, so this research is urgent.

It is also noticeable from research conducted into the scope and aims of these partnerships for this book that not one of the listed projects dealt with the digital-creative and cultural industries. Given the central role that these industries are playing in global economic growth and trade, and their undoubted value to the

SAMOA Pathway goal of Sustained and Sustainable, Inclusive and Equitable Economic Growth and Decent Work for All, this is a worrying but not wholly surprising oversight.

Alongside this, a positive step towards a more implementable solution for public–private partnership for the SDGs would be more clearly defined roles for the private sector. Whilst the private sector is mentioned in many of the partnership statements and research documents around SDG delivery, it is often vague, lacking in concrete proposals and often limited in the understanding of private sector strengths and capabilities. It is also noticeable that grassroots and community groups also have limited participation in these partnerships (Clough et al., 2019).

To bring about a connected approach that links the macro levels of partnership strategy to the micro and local levels of the dynamics of delivery, the private sector has to be empowered to innovate, particularly in the digital-creative-knowledge economy, and to bring a committed entrepreneurial drive to delivering market solutions to the goals. Whilst national government and international organisations can provide useful structures and targeted fiscal instruments, it is the impact of localised solutions with high social and community uptake that will actually deliver real results on the ground.

SDG delivery is not about strategy, policy and broad statements of good intent but ultimately about the everyday lives of people and communities and the products and services that are used. Without their engagement, in a coordinated bottom-up and top-down process, the decade of delivery will struggle to make real progress. Partnerships therefore have to be embedded in communities and be accountable to them.

This also has to not just be about a revised CSR statement for the private sector – seeing the list of sustainable goals in a company's statement is not progress on the delivery of those goals. The whole private sector from MSMEs to multinational corporations has to see the market value in developing products and services that work in harmony with national and local policy, overarching strategic plans and global finance (BSDC, 2017).

The perceived antagonism of corporations and international finance to sustainability no longer holds true in the way in which it did even just two or three years ago. The market now sees the value of products with environmental and sustainable credentials, and investors are increasingly seeing impact as a key factor behind investment decisions (Barclays Bank, 2018).

Unfortunately, the perceived wisdom, or more accurately ideology, that capitalism is incompatible with sustainable development, still holds true in many NGO and academic circles. The assumption that only governments can deliver the SDGs is important to counter if they are indeed to be in any way deliverable.

Because in practice, each country has responsibility and sovereignty for its own development and the implementation of the SDGs, it is the global private sector that has the greatest ability to actually deliver these goals. National governments, although seen by many as having the responsibility to deliver the SDGs, are volatile, susceptible to swings in political ideology and hence unreliable as custodians of this responsibility. The withdrawal of the United States from the Paris Climate agreement is a prime example of that tendency.

Governments and organisations like the United Nations then can contribute by facilitating international FDI flows, research support mechanisms and ministerial cooperation, but ultimately they need to target all this support towards innovation and entrepreneurship at a national and sub-national level. It is products and services, used by and engaged with the local populations, not high-level strategies and global forums, that will deliver the SDGs. Unfortunately, that message, at present, seems to be getting lost.

The role of the private sector in delivering the SDGs

At the Sustainable Development Goals Summit in 2019, the UN Secretary General called on all parts of society to come together, to act and to deliver the decade of action through three levels of action: through global action to bring leadership, resources and innovation to the SDGs; through local action to embed change in the policies, regulatory frameworks, finance and institutions; and through people action to engage young people, the wider civil society, the media, private sector and academia to deliver real transformations.

It is interesting to see where the whole global trade and economic system is placed in that call, not as part of global action, leadership or regional or local economies, but as part of the call around people. One might see from this that despite a number of statements around the importance of the private sector to the SDGs, there is still something of a relegation of industry to the 'and also' category.

Current private sector activity in support of the SDGs tends to fall into one of two categories. First, there are the now widely embraced actions to report on aspects of corporate sustainable development performance, with KPMG (2017) noting that around 90% of the world's largest companies now take part. Second is the action of private sector finance in supporting the 2030 Agenda, which is discussed in more detail in the chapter on island entrepreneurship.

What is missing from many discussions of, and research into, private sector involvement in sustainable development is the role of SMEs and the importance of collaborative connections between industry sectors, such as the obvious importance of the digital-creative sectors to innovation in established industries of real importance to SIDS, such as tourism and healthcare. These connections and opportunities are not articulated in any real way, and this then has an impact on the ability to deliver innovative solutions in practice on the ground.

So key to a truly engaged and collaborative public–private sector partnership for the SDGs has to be a remodelled multi-stakeholder and multi-sector approach. There has to be a much greater emphasis on the role of the whole private sector, which encompasses not only large corporations and private finance but also local MSMEs, entrepreneurs and innovators that can work collaboratively and connectively to find solutions to the regression that is happening in many of the SDG goals.

Much of this positive action around the SDGs can come from simply supporting the digital-creative economy and its strong sustainable growth capabilities to grow and engage with other sectors, such as the Blue Economy in SIDS. There is not necessarily a requirement to badge this as an SDG project, or to burden it with specific expectations around any particular goal, which can be problematic for small companies.

There is urgency in developing the engagement of the private sector and the currently underused and undervalued digital-creative MSME potential in SDG delivery. There is of course the pressure on national and sub-national governments to invest human and fiscal resources into the 2030 Agenda at a time when the Covid-19 pandemic and the resultant global recession have put many economies in considerable trouble – none more so than those of SIDS.

If these governments are struggling to adequately deliver on their SDG commitments, then it is vital that international organisations and the United Nations in particular take a much greater role not just in leading strategy and convening all possible partners but in facilitating practical delivery with these underused sectors. It can do this by greater support on the ground with entrepreneurs in the cities, countries and regions that will be the focus of the goals.

To do this the UN will require greater support both financially and institutionally, and the private sector, particularly those larger multinational companies, must step up with this support so that it can be a facilitator both at an overall strategic level and as an on-the-ground enabler.

An example of this might be companies like Google or Amazon working with seed and start-up entrepreneurs in small island states to build local, regional and then global e-commerce or content platform systems that can see both specialised outward trade and inward investment. This contributes to better high-value jobs and skills and builds sustainable and low environmental impact economies. These local entrepreneurs can then mentor the next generation of innovators and contribute to the growth of post-secondary education.

This latter point can then be delivered in partnership with UNESCO and funded through regionally focused VC and Angel funds, established through a corporate impact investing scheme. We then see how international organisations, large multinational corporations and local start-up or growth-stage entrepreneurs can drive progress on the SDGs. We have to move away from prioritising and overly pressurising the public sector as the key in this mission because, as we've seen, it is manifestly not working.

This move to a greater engagement of the breadth of the private sector and industry sectors such as the digital-creative and cultural industries then has the potential to accelerate the necessary transformations by developing and implementing greater cross-sector synergies and innovation (Sachs et al., 2019).

The work of Nilsson et al. (2016) in mapping the interactions and interdependencies between the SDGs shows just how important this cross-sector, connected and collaborative innovation and implementation is if the 2030 Agenda is to be successful.

So whilst it is easy to point the finger at national governments and the United Nations for their perceived failings, the answer is not to simply do more of and put greater resource into what has already been done but to look at innovative partnerships, working models and greater sectoral connectedness to make the necessary progress in SDG implementation.

It is also of real importance to examine how greater connectedness between the Goals can be achieved so that they can work in harmony and not in conflict with one another. Stafford-Smith et al. (2017) argue that the implementation targets are largely silent about interlinkages and interdependencies among goals, regardless of their ambition to be "universal, indivisible, and interlinked" (clause 71).

The concepts of the Triple Helix can be central here in delivering the SDGs, engaging a networked group of actors such as national government, private sector, civil society and international agencies to not only build partnerships but also innovate in interlinking these partnerships and goals. However, as we'll see from the later chapter on redefining the Helix, there is work to be done here also in rethinking how the dynamics and structures of these relations can work for a hugely dynamic and uncertain economy, particularly in SIDS.

The impact of this dynamic uncertainty on these universal goals will, as we've already seen with the effects on levels of poverty, create significant inertia to progress unless governments and, more importantly, non-government actors mobilise effectively to ensure that they are actually implemented. However, this mobilisation will again be ineffectual if the direction of travel is unclear and is guided by restrictive strategic thinking that lacks true innovation.

That innovation is essential as the Goals are hugely ambitious, seen by some commentators as being unrealistic to the point of fantasy and not sufficiently taking into account the extreme heterogeneity of national governments' priorities and political ideologies. The SDGs, targeted to be delivered by 2030, are having to work against a world reeling from the Covid-19 pandemic and a global population that is expected to reach 8.5 billion by that time. India is projected to overtake China as the world's most populous country before then, and Nigeria would become the third-largest country by population by 2050. At that point, half the world's population will be concentrated in nine countries: India, Nigeria, Pakistan, the Democratic Republic of the Congo, Ethiopia, Tanzania, the United States, Indonesia and Uganda (United Nations, 2015).

This heaps huge pressure on the already struggling SDG project, and if the partnership and implementation strategies for the SDGs are not overhauled in a radical way, then they will certainly fail.

Amongst all the challenges and often negative press around the SDGs, there is an important point to make here though. Whilst achieving the global goals may not happen as envisaged, it is the process of collaborative and concerted action, energy and commitment that is taken towards getting there that is just as valuable.

In this case, we could understand the SDGs as being formative, not summative.

The digital-creative economy and the SDGs

The United Nations Development Programme recognises the importance of the cultural and creative industries as a driver of human development, particularly as they empower people to take ownership and responsibility for their own development (Palanivel, 2019).

The CCI are generally more inclusive than other industries, with high levels of youth and women engaged in these sectors in both developed countries and the developing world (UNCTAD, 2018).

As we've seen in previous chapters, the new technologies of production and distribution have accelerated cooperation and trade in creative and cultural goods between nations and across the Global North and South. However, the creative economy is also one of the most unevenly distributed industries, with Europe and North America accounting for 93% of global CCI revenue and 85% of all CCI jobs worldwide (UNCTAD, 2018).

There is some progress on this front though, with China, the Middle East and Africa enacting programmes and initiatives focused on building and capitalising on the strength of creative talent in their respective regions. The International Centre for Creativity and Sustainable Development (ICCSD) in Beijing is a new international think tank for creativity development. It has launched CREATIV-ITY 2030 (C2030), a new global initiative which seeks to stimulate, mobilise and exchange creative solutions, tools and approaches in all walks of life.

Both Dubai and Abu Dhabi have committed resources to the development of creative industry support, in terms of both local infrastructure and international partnerships, and in January 2020, the African Export-Import Bank, Afreximbank, announced a US$500 million credit facility to support African cultural and creative products and producers over the following two years (Afreximbank, 2020).

The untapped potential for digital-creative economies across the globe though is significant, as the aforementioned initiatives remain limited and are often isolated from broader economic policy, whether national or regional. When it comes to SIDS, that situation is even more pronounced. The Caribbean has made some strides to implementing both regional and national creative economy support; the Caribbean Development Bank's Creative and Cultural Innovation Fund is a good example of this, but concerted and collaborative action is still very limited.

This is a real challenge for SIDS, as building and sustaining a vibrant creative economy requires connected action across many different policy areas, such as education, labour markets, technology infrastructure, public and private finance markets, and macroeconomic policies. The dominance of the Blue Economy across these policy and strategy areas relegates action on CCI to a significantly lower priority.

Whilst this might be understandable given the importance of sectors such as tourism to these regions, it is the ability of the creative economy though to act, collaborate and innovate across all industry sectors and the 17 SDGs that make the digital-creative and cultural industries so dynamic and so vital to SIDS and the 2030 Agenda.

The United Nations has been active in promoting the CCI, bringing together UNESCO, UNCTAD and UNDP together through a series of meetings, reports and research. The UNCTAD has an established Creative Economy Programme, and I was fortunate to be able to present some of the research from this book at the Creative Economy Expert Group meeting in Geneva in October 2019.

The issue then seems to be not the will to establish creative economies in developing regions but rather a practical and on-the-ground connecting of this work on creative economies to the broader global trends of digital and technological development and applying that to developing regions, particularly SIDS.

Siloed and traditional approaches to this still abound, and there is work to be done to help governments and key organisations understand the digital technology-creative industries' cross-sector opportunities for regional and sub-regional development and its implementation.

Despite all the positive data around the global creative industries, from both an economic and social standpoint, and the broad understanding of the importance of these sectors, there is still a noticeable and concerning lack of research on the role of creative economies in achieving the SDGs. This then translates into an absence of direct action on the ground to put the statements and declarations on the digital-creative and cultural industries into practice. This is surprising given the global dynamism of the digital-creative industries and its transformational impact on global trade.

An example of this lack is the website of the International Institute for Sustainable Development (www.iisd.org), an independent think tank on sustainability solutions with a motto of Delivering the Knowledge to Act. If one searches its articles, research documents and blogs for 'creative industries' or 'creative economies', not a single document that addresses those topics is returned. What is ironic is that the focus of their work is entitled the CREATE Strategy.

This is not entirely surprising or uncommon as the focus of research and action around the SDGs is very much on the traditional topics of water, environment, climate and so on, with the primacy of technology, science and policy very much to the fore. The alignment is with the titles of the individual SDGs themselves, but if the last few years have taught us anything, and especially now, this approach to achieving the SDGs and to making the 'decade of action' a concrete deliverable needs a fundamental, more inclusive rethink.

There is a desperate need for innovation in how countries, research institutions and international organisations approach this task, a need to connect these goals to a far wider set of economic, social and cultural actors and to engage in a more entrepreneurial approach to their implementation. This begins with the research and development of delivery mechanisms and transfers into local, national and international policy and strategy.

Vlassis (2016) puts forward three factors that explain why the CCIs remain marginalised within the international development agenda and hence the SDGs themselves: first, the fragmented nature of UNESCO strategies; second, the reluctance of developed countries to recognise the importance of the CCIs in delivering sustainable development; third, a top-down approach to policy that lacks a strong transnational mobilisation of CCI organisations.

Whilst points two and three certainly hold some truth, the critique of UNESCO's strategies may actually be more down to a structural, rather than a strategic, failing. The organisation is not helped by a precarious financial situation and a remit that is far too broad to be actually achievable and impactful in any meaningful way. Any organisation that is nominally responsible for the global development of education, science and culture is always going to struggle to make headway.

What is clear is that the key remit of UNESCO to deliver on SDG 4 – inclusive and equitable quality education for all – is under severe strain, making it all the more unusual then that it has cut its education budget for 2020–2021 to just 15% of its annual total budget. Inevitably then, the focus on CCI as part of the whole SDG catalogue is going to suffer.

This sidelining of CCI as a real driver of sustainable development and a force for achieving the SDGs, although certainly not intentional, appears systemic, on a national government and an international organisation level. If progress is to be made, then it is the private sector that must take the lead in innovating the products and approaches and the implementation of the 2030 Agenda.

The importance of the creative economy

The creative, digital and innovation economy should not just be limited to the developed world. Indeed, for developing regions it is absolutely essential to see these sectors playing an increasingly important role in the national economic mix. For SIDS in particular, this digital-creative economy can be crucial to the successful achievement of many of the UN's SDGs. We can see that directly in terms of SDGs 12, Responsible consumption and production, 13, Climate action, and 14, Life below water.

Alongside this, the impact that a thriving creative economy has on innovation across sectors cannot be overestimated, with a corresponding impact then on the successful delivery across all SDGs. As described in the previous chapter, the pressure on the Blue Economy and the health of the oceans are of critical importance to SIDS and to the SDGs in general.

The issue of over-reliance on the Blue Economy and the narrow economic bases for SIDS has of course been highlighted in the restrictions placed upon tourism by the Covid-19 pandemic. There is no doubt that the Blue economy will remain the most important sector for SIDS, as well as one of the most important areas of required action for global economic inclusion, sustainability and equality over the next decade. However, the Blue Economy has to fulfil its ultimate remit – it has to be not just sustainable but ultimately environmentally positive.

With almost 50% of the world's population predicted to be in the countries of the Indian Ocean Rim by 2050 (Doyle, 2018), the reality of sustainable use of our oceans is a long way off unless we think and act in a more innovative and cross-sectoral way. Statements and declarations have to translate into innovation and impact. This can only be achieved if the Blue Economy is seen as part of a whole and not the whole in itself. From that then we can see that delivering the SDGs must be truly multi-sector and cross-sector and driven by strong public–private partnerships (Schroeder, 2019).

Whilst progress has been made on sustainable development in these regions, the island tourism industry, for example, is making great strides in sustainable practices such as the elimination of plastic waste, water conservation and local food production; it is still hugely impactful in terms of carbon footprint, is founded on a generally low-skill and low-paid local or migrant workforce, and the majority of the profits do not stay in the regions in which they are generated (Akadiri et al., 2019). So whilst some of the SDGs are being worked on positively in SIDS, others are seemingly being missed out or not addressed in a coherent and connected fashion.

The Covid-19 pandemic has generated a number of discussions on how these negative impacts on tourism can be reduced, with the shift to fewer numbers and higher values being the prime message. This is easier said than done though with a variety of stakeholders with competing interests all seeking to recover from the current crisis in their own way.

The key of course is to engender cross-sector innovation and multi-sector strategic development. The more isolated the emphasis placed on the development of the Blue Economy in SIDS, for example, and the more focus, energy and research conducted solely in this discipline without connection to other sectors, the more pressure is placed upon it to achieve its goal of sustainable economic growth. That, unfortunately, is where it and the SGDs have the prospect of falling down, with the pressure to deliver growth, as the population grows to around 8.5 billion by 2030, overriding progress on sustainability in practice and on the ground in those communities.

To avoid this it is important to see sustainable development in SIDS regions, and the wider delivery of the SDGs, as a holistic whole, placing an emphasis on digital, creative and knowledge-based economic drivers just as much as on traditional routes to sustainable development, such as the Blue Economy or clean energy. We then have the possibility of not just maintaining but improving the health of the environment and the oceans, of delivering greater equity and inclusion in sustainable economic growth, and of engaging society and culture in the whole mix (Halpern et al., 2019).

With the global economic system facing greater uncertainty, pressure and upheaval than at any time in the last 100 years, the impact of these forces on delivering sustainable development will only increase. For small island states then in particular, this dynamic uncertainty means they have to innovate in their thinking around the sectors in which they invest and in the policy and strategic frameworks that their governments put in place.

This is why the digital-creative-knowledge economy will be so important to these regions and to the SDGs as a whole. The vulnerabilities of all developing countries have now come into sharp focus with the economic upheaval and uncertainty that is all too present at this time. The development models that were widely accepted just last year have all been called into question, and the urge to 'build back better' can only happen if we look beyond the traditionally accepted theories and strategies.

That argument still has some way to go in terms of acceptance and even understanding by developing country governments and key international groups, with 'creative industries' still often seen simply as arts and cultural heritage and consigned to footnotes or single-line entries at the end of economic development strategies. This is despite the numerous conferences, strategies, white papers and forums happening around the world on the benefits to the economy of supporting creative and cultural entrepreneurs.

The real issue is the understanding that strong creative economies are not just found in the major cities of the developed world. Briguglio (2014) makes an interesting observation that for small island states there is almost a neo-colonial attitude around the creative industries and the ability of SIDS to build sustainable creative economies, harking back to the scholars of the 1960s and their presumption of the economic non-viability that surrounded that period's wave of island state sovereignty. The research and work around the sustainability of SIDS is a prime example of this.

Despite virtually unanimous agreement on the need to broaden island economies to ameliorate the impacts of climate and economic shocks, and their vulnerability in terms of distance from markets, economies of scale and lack of natural resource beyond the oceans, those propounding the opportunities that the digital-creative economies present still struggle to be heard and to be taken seriously. The support then for island-based creative entrepreneurs is severely limited.

The UN SAMOA Pathway document called upon the international community to support SIDS in designing and implementing their own innovative cultural policies to strengthen heritage and creativity and leverage the economic, social and natural benefits of culture (UN, 2014).

The 'creative industries' were mentioned in that section, but it is revealing to see how it is contextualised and aligned. The document highlights preserving tangible and intangible cultural heritage and promoting culture for island sustainable development, which is certainly important, but again there is a failure to understand that creative industries, as a tool for sustainable development, are far wider than just cultural heritage.

For example, there was no mention of the development of digital exports – the fastest growing global export sector and something which circumvents the well-worn distance-to-markets argument. There was no discussion of the alignment of creative and cultural products and producers to international e-commerce systems – a market that is now worth more than $26 trillion and that makes up 30% of global GDP (UNCTAD, 2017). With the remaking of the economic model post-Covid-19, that figure is set to grow substantially.

Computer games design and production, film and television production, digital design, mobile content and data platforms, visual effects and immersive technology are the key drivers of the explosion of creative industries as a global economic success story. The computer games industry, for instance, is worth around

$165 billion, with significant growth estimated for 2020 and 2021 (Gough, 2018). Yet these are conspicuous by their absence from discussions of creative industries and sustainable development in small island states; the belief, of course, is that these sectors belong in the major cities of the developed world and can't be part of the economic mix of small island states in any meaningful way. That, however, belies the nature of the business.

Key to the value of these industries to SIDS is their ability to circumvent many of the traditional difficulties and vulnerabilities associated with small island states. The games sector, for example, has no reliance on exploiting natural resources; it bypasses the need to distribute physical goods, so distance from markets is not an issue; and its growth is not restricted by small domestic markets as it can sell directly to a global audience instantly. It can work both B2B and B2C and can engage in cross-sectoral innovation through gamification and serious games applications.

Games start-ups have the ability to scale quickly, with a total consumer market currently standing at over 2.5 billion games users and growing fast as smartphone penetration accelerates (Gough, 2019). With the global number of internet-connected devices expected to reach 50 billion by 2030, the demand for creative content is only going to increase (Statista, 2020). Combine that with the roll-out of 5G networks in island regions such as the Caribbean, Maldives and Seychelles, and this sector is emerging as a true global economic powerhouse that can locate almost anywhere in the world.

This just gives an example of a digital-creative sector that has enormous potential to work successfully in small island states and be a real force in delivering SDGs around inclusive economic development and decent jobs. What is required, of course, is the foresight to put in place the structures to make it happen – education, start-up ecosystems, investment opportunities and cluster networks to support companies in the initial years of growth and then give them the means and structures to expand.

One significant barrier to making this happen is the perception of the CCI in the development sector, government departments and the sustainable development research community. Papers and reviews of the SAMOA Pathway by researchers and agencies in the Caribbean note the importance of the creative, or Orange Economy, but, as mentioned earlier, it is revealing to see how that is discussed. The Association of Caribbean States (ACS) recognises that the creative economy can be a significant engine for sustainable development in the region but then highlights the carnival sector as simply a way of growing further tourism revenue and sees arts and crafts industries as a way of diversifying the tourist experience (Dubrie et al., 2019).

These are both valid reasons to support those creative sectors, reinforcing the points made earlier about the ability of creative industries to drive cross-sector growth. It is noteworthy, however, that the creative sector is framed primarily as a way of growing tourism and not as a significant sector in its own right. This links back to the pathway document statements around tangible and intangible cultural heritage.

The majority of impacts that the creative industries have had on the global economic and trade systems have come because of their transformation through digital technology. So whilst the objectives in the SAMOA Pathway document recognise that CCI are important to the economic and social well-being of SIDS, it is the lack of connecting this, literally and conceptually, to the opportunities of technological and digital transformation that has held them back, and continues to do so.

This is, of course, of critical importance now given the collapse of the tourist industry in island states across the world. The scale of the Covid-19 impact on global tourism is outlined in a UNWTO report (UNWTO, 2020) that predicts a decline in international arrivals of between 58% and 80% this year.

It threatens the livelihoods of up to 120 million people who directly rely on tourism – with vastly more than that indirectly – and looks set to cause a loss of export revenues of up to US$1 trillion. Proportionally though, of course, the impact on small island states is far worse than for larger developed countries in Europe or the Americas. Island states and the wider developing world simply don't have the economic muscle to throw money at the problem to temporarily prop up jobs and companies.

The importance then of the digital-creative sectors is in their ability to build strong, high-skill, high-wage sectors in themselves and to contribute to innovation and value-added growth in every other sector. For SIDS, this can no longer be left as a strategic footnote.

Conclusion

As has been said widely, there can be no return to normal – we have to start designing now the kind of new normal we want. The importance on delivering the promise of the SDGs and the 2030 Agenda is greater than ever, but so are the challenges and downward pressures. Global poverty levels have gone backwards, the oceans are increasingly acidic and biodiversity is under a greater threat than ever before.

Not returning to normal has to also apply then to how we approach all the elements of the sustainable development agenda. The methods, strategies, partnerships and financing of the SDGs all need radical overhaul if they are to have any real meaning.

For SIDS, that has to be an economy with a broader base, that allows local MSMEs to reach global markets and bring significant revenue home, that is driven by knowledge-based, creative digital skills and business models, and that drives innovation across every other sector.

Recognition of the CCI then, particularly those driven by digital technology, is crucial to the process of designing and implementing more resilient and locally driven entrepreneurial economies and making sure this 'decade of delivery' on the SDGs does not stall before it has even got going.

To address these highly dynamic and complex challenges will require a much greater understanding and implementation of the opportunities and strengths of a digital-creative, knowledge-based economy allied to the technologies of the Fourth Industrial Revolution. The SDGs cannot be delivered by science and technology alone, and the creative economy, so central to establishing and driving innovation, has to be a key element of the delivery of the 2030 Agenda. So it is more than just a case of making the CCI part of the economic fabric of a country. It is recognising that the conditions faced by both developing and developed nations in acting to deliver the SDGs require the skills and knowledge that only the creative industries can provide.

By moving the argument on sustainable, equitable and inclusive growth towards a multi-sector and cross-sector development model, the opportunities to engage the creative entrepreneurial drive of island peoples not only start to be possible but also really make economic sense.

References

Afreximbank. 2020. Afreximbank Announces $500 Million Creative Industry Support Fund as CAX WKND Opens. Press release, January 17. Accessed at www.afreximbank.com/afreximbank-announces-$500-million-creative-industry-support- fund-as-cax-wknd-opens.

Akadiri, A.C., Akadiri, S.S. & Alola, U.J. 2019. Is There Growth Impact of Tourism? Evidence from Selected Small Island States. *Current Issues in Tourism*, 22(12), pp. 1480–1498.

Barclays Bank. 2018. *Investor Motivations for Impact: A Behavioural Examination*. Barclays Bank, London.

Briguglio, L. 2014. *A Vulnerability and Resilience Framework for Small States. Book Chapter in, Building the Resilience of Small States*. Commonwealth Secretariat, London.

Business and Sustainable Development Commission. 2017. *Better Business Better World: The Report of the Business and Sustainable Development Commission*. Business and Sustainable Development Commission, London.

Carson, R. 1962. *Silent Spring*. Houghton Mifflin, Boston, MA.

Clough, E., Long, G. & Rietig, K.A. 2019. Study of Partnerships and Initiatives Registered on the UNSDG Partnerships Platform. In *An Independent Report Commission by the United Nations Department for Economic and Social Affairs (UNDESA)*. UNDESA, New York, NY.

Dodds, F. 2015. *Multi-Stakeholder Partnerships: Making Them Work for the Post-2015 Development Agenda*. ECOSOC/United Nations, New York, NY.

D'Orville, H. 2019. The Relationship between Sustainability and Creativity. *CADMUS*, 4(1), October, pp. 65–73.

Doyle, T. 2018. Blue Economy and the Indian Ocean Rim. *Journal of the Indian Ocean Region*, 14(1), pp. 1–6.

Dubrie, A., Thorne, E., Fontes de Meira, L., Bello, O. & Phillips, W. 2019. Synthesis of the Caribbean Subregion Midterm Review of the Small Island Developing States Accelerated Modalities of Action Pathway. *Studies and Perspectives*, 83. ECLAC.

Gough, C. 2018. *Value of the Global Video Games Market 2012–2021*. Statista. Accessed at www.statista.com/246888.

Gough, C. 2019. *Number of Video Gamers Worldwide 2014–2021*. Statista. Accessed at www.statista.com/748044.

Halpern, B.S., Frazier, M., Afflerbach, J., et al. 2019. Recent Pace of Change in Human Impact on the World's Ocean. *Scientific Reports*, 9(1).

KPMG. 2017. *Survey of Corporate Responsibility Reporting*. KPMG Netherlands, Amstelveen.

Meadows, D.H., Meadows, D.L., Randers, J. & Behrens, W. 1972. *The Limits to Growth; A Report for the Club of Rome's Project on the Predicament of Mankind*. Universe Books, New York, NY.

Nilsson, M., Griggs, D. & Visbeck, M. 2016. Policy: Map the Interactions between Sustainable Development Goals. *Nature*, 534, pp. 320–322. International Council for Science. A Draft Framework for Understanding SDG Interactions ICSU: 2016. Accessed at http://bit.ly/sdg-interactions.

Palanivel, T. 2019. *How Cultural and Creative Industries Can Power Human Development in the 21st Century*. UNDP. Accessed at http://hdr.undp.org/en/content/how-cultural-and-creative-industries-can-power-human-development-21st-century.

Sachs, J., Schmidt-Traub, G., Kroll, C., Lafortune, G. & Fuller, G. 2019. *Sustainable Development Report 2019; Bertelsmann Stiftung and Sustainable Development Solutions Network (SDSN)*. Sustainable Development Solutions Network, New York, NY.

Schroeder, C.J. 2019. *Sustainably Leveraging the Blue Economy Through Public-Private Partnerships: A Case Study of Namibia's Port Development*. World Maritime University, Malmo.

Stafford-Smith, M., Griggs, D., Gaffney, O., Ullah, F., Reyers, B., Kanie, N., Stigson, B., Shrivastava, P., Leach, M. & O'Connell, D. 2017. Integration: The Key to Implementing the Sustainable Development Goals. *Sustainability Science*, 12(6), pp. 911–919.

Statista Research Department. 2020. IoT Connected Devices Worldwide 2030. Accessed at www.statista.com/802690.

United Nations. 2014. *SIDS Accelerated Modalities of Action (SAMOA) Pathway*. Resolution document A/RES/69/15. United Nations, New York, NY.

United Nations. 2015. *Transforming our World: The 2030 Agenda for Sustainable Development. In Outcome Document for the United Nations Summit to Adopt the Post 2015 Development Agenda*. United Nations, New York, NY.

United Nations. 2018. *Resolution A/RES/73/254. Towards Global Partnerships: A Principle Based Approach to Enhanced Cooperation between the United Nations and All Relevant Partners*. United Nations, New York, NY.

United Nations Conference on Environment and Development. Rio de Janerio, Brazil, 3rd to 14th June 1992. p3 1.1.

United Nations Conference on Trade and Development. 2017. *The New Digital Economy and Development*. Technical Note No.8. UNCTAD, Geneva.

United Nations Conference on Trade and Development. 2018. *Creative Economy Outlook: Trends in International Trade in Creative Industries 2002–2015*. UNCTAD, Geneva.

United Nations Small Island Developing States Action Platform. Accessed September 2020 at https://sidspartnerships.un.org/partnerships.

United Nations World Tourism Organisation. 2020. *World Tourism Barometer and Statistical Annex, January 2020*. UNWTO, Madrid.

Vlassis, A. 2016. UNESCO, Cultural Industries and the International Development Agenda. In Stupples, P. & Teaiwa, K. (Eds.), *Contemporary Perspectives on Art and International Development*, pp. 48–61. Taylor & Francis, London.

World Commission on Environment and Development. 1987. *Our Common Future*. Oxford University Press, Oxford.

3 Small Island Developing States and the Fourth Industrial Revolution

Introduction

Two hundred and fifty years ago, the invention of a reliable steam-powered engine began the process of mechanising production, spurred the growth of cities and led to unprecedented societal transformation. That First Industrial Revolution was followed by the creation of new energy forms in oil and electricity that defined the Second Industrial Revolution, eventually leading on to the digital technologies of computers, the internet and mobile phones that characterised the Third Industrial Revolution.

We are now entering another revolution, one that could be more significant and more transformative than any that have gone before.

The Fourth Industrial Revolution (4IR) is defined by the next generation of these digital technologies, such as AI, blockchain, immersive technologies and big data. It is witnessing applications in autonomous vehicles, smart cities, digital content production and distribution and enabling unprecedented cross-sector innovation and collaboration. Perhaps, the greatest impact of this revolution, however, maybe its sustainability.

Previous industrial revolutions have had considerable and largely damaging effects on the environment that we have only recently realised the scale of. As the population is predicted to hit close to 9 billion people by 2050, with a commensurate increase in the consumption of food, materials and energy, this next industrial revolution has to reverse the huge and damaging exploitation of natural resources and environments.

The ability to create value, wealth and meaningful jobs through digital production and distribution is a significant element of this revolution. The technology is there and is evolving rapidly. The challenge now is to put in place the governance, education, research, policy and financial frameworks to make this digital-creative economy more sustainable, equitable and evenly spread than any previous incarnation.

Accelerating change

Although these revolutions have been defined by technological innovation, with perhaps the 4IR being the most technology focused in terms of how it is discussed, the real legacy of these changes have been their impacts on society and culture and the disruption caused by the changes in economies and livelihoods. They challenged governments to understand and respond to unprecedented changes and put considerable strain on social and cultural systems (UNCTAD, 2019).

What we are seeing now, more than in any previous generations are the technological and economic revolutions of the past becoming a continual and ever more rapid disruptive evolutionary flow.

The pace of technology change now is so fast that societies, education and skills and regulatory frameworks are struggling to keep up. The roll-out of 5G communication networks around the world will have considerable impact on every aspect of economic and social life – but could be gone before the end of the decade to be replaced by 6G, with exponential increase in data speeds, disruptions and applications.

Research is also already underway on quantum communications that will in turn supersede 6G speeds by as yet unknown multiples. This increase in communication speeds is expected to see global mobile data traffic growing by 55% annually between 2020 and 2030 and generate 5016 exabyte of data per month by 2030 (Nawaz et al., 2019).

These accelerating changes to lives, businesses and societies are posing new risks and raising significant ethical concerns (Mpofu & Nicolaides, 2019). There are also a number of issues around the impact of new and developing technologies on privacy, democracy and equality.

For developing countries these industrial revolutions are in many instances merging and occurring simultaneously, creating industrial manufacturing structures and urban developments similar to the Second Industrial Revolution, whilst at the same time rolling out the fast internet connections, mobile banking and cashless transactions of the Third Revolution. Now, alongside this, the 4IR is often being implemented faster than in some developing countries (Bandura et al., 2019).

So this leapfrogging of the phases of past industrial development is seeing many developing regions implement better and faster technology infrastructure and applications than some developed countries. This offers the opportunity for these developing countries to move from just being consumers of technology and content to producers and exporters. The implications for delivering growth and particularly around the delivery of the SDGs are profound.

This economic and technological growth continues however to be uneven, with many left behind. Wage stagnation, jobless growth, environmental challenges and migration are not only posing challenges but also creating significant opportunities, particularly for women and girls who could see greater opportunity and empowerment through equitable access to technology and innovation (Kamal & Diksha, 2019). For developing countries then, the focus needs to be not just enabling technological uptake and implementation but making it human-centred, sustainable and equitable.

For SIDS, and developing regions more widely, the impact of these 4IR technologies could be profound. However, it is important to realise that for these regions, with a strong need to develop sustainably, it is not just changing up what is already there, in reworking large-scale manufacturing or in making traditional industries more efficient, for example, but in allowing these regions to open up entirely new avenues for entrepreneurship, creative innovation and collaboration in new sectors. The reason for this is that technology has changed the global industrial and trade landscape.

Industry in transition

The world's developed economies have seen a fundamental shift away from the old industrial model to a new one based on creativity and knowledge. In place of the natural resource-intensive, large-scale manufacturing industries that defined previous decades, economic growth today is increasingly powered by creative innovation, digital technology and talent.

This is not the marketing spin of technology companies or the predictions of commentators and journalists. The global market provides the simplest and most dramatic way of showing this revolution – through the way it values businesses. The first decade of this Millennium was dominated by commodity-based companies, principally in the extractive sector, such as ExxonMobil, ConoccoPhillips and Chevron Corporation, along with automotive and some retail, namely Walmart (Fortune Magazine, 2019).

Less than ten years later, none of those corporations were in the top five most valuable companies by market capitalisation. Instead, they were replaced exclusively by technology companies – Amazon, Google, Microsoft, Apple and Facebook. Apple alone is now worth more than the entire US energy sector, putting into perspective how those former giants of the early 2000s have been dwarfed by the rise of technology companies (Financial Times, 2019).

That remarkable change has taken less than a decade. The speed of industrial change is accelerating, and there is seemingly no terminal velocity to this change. This new industrial revolution is now disrupting every sector, from healthcare and finance to manufacturing, tourism and education. However, nowhere has that transformational impact been so profound as on the cultural and creative industries. For content producers, production costs have fallen, distribution has become truly ubiquitous and new technologies have opened up previously unthinkable applications. The creative industries have gone from cottage industry to global economic powerhouse.

The UK, for example, has a global reputation as a leader in the creative industries with the world's third most valuable creative sector – behind the United States and China. In 2018, £111 billion was added to the UK's economy, thanks to the creative industries (DCMS, 2020). That is four times the gross value added of the automotive industry, six times as much as life sciences and nearly ten times that of aerospace. The creative economy, in all its forms, has become the leading edge of economic development, growth and change. The power behind that rise of the creative industries has been the Third and now Fourth Industrial Revolutions.

The changing face of export-led growth

Developing regions and countries have often seen the growth of export volume as a way to grow economies, using large-scale off-shore manufacturing developments and special economic zones to scale up exports and foreign exchange revenues. Sometimes, however, this can be to the detriment of strong national, sustainable economies and knowledge-based skills development (Ling-yee & Ogunmokun, 2015), with these sizeable manufacturing facilities requiring a large and constant supply of mainly low-skill and low-value labour.

In the age of the 4IR, however, that global trade is changing. Developing countries in particular are starting to see the impact of these technologies on manufacturing, employment and economic development.

If the mobilisation of cheap labour, as the main competitive advantage of many developing countries to grow and accumulate capital is becoming less and less of an advantage, then governments need to refocus on building creative, digital and knowledge-based economies that can sit alongside, support and eventually replace these traditional lower-skilled economies. At a macro level, the emergence of the 4IR will see labour demand reducing, manufacturing returning to the locations of consumption and the lowering of income and consumption in already low-income countries. Malkawi (2019) suggests that we could see a substantial slowdown in the international trade in tangible goods because of the impact of these technologies on developing country labour markets.

So, this well-tried and tested model of traditional, export-led growth could start to lose momentum, most importantly for the standard growth model for uplifting developing countries. If this is the case, then developing countries need to find other ways of growing, diversifying and making sustainable their economies. And that is the key point – the traditional model is no longer suitable if we want to develop sustainable economies in developing countries and SIDS in particular. The rise of digital-creative industries as a major economic force globally opens up the possibility to reshape that old model along entirely different lines.

These digital-creative industries are generating new opportunities for trade, growth and entrepreneurship, allowing creators to reach global audiences through platforms such as Amazon Appstore, Google Play, YouTube, Facebook, Patreon and Steam. Creative businesses and entrepreneurs are leading the way in digital innovation, utilising these new technologies to open up new frictionless B2B and B2C international trade routes. In the context of a highly globalised, fast-growing technological landscape, it is important not to overlook these digital exports. The way the market values companies and its products clearly indicates just how dramatically that global trade is shifting (OECD, 2019).

This has particular importance for SIDS in that digital trade and exports present an opportunity for economic growth without the usual limitations of geography or natural resources discussed in the previous chapter. It also provides a sustainable, high-skill and high-wage growth strategy that can engage young people in ways that traditional industries in these regions have failed to do. It can also do something to halt the decline of island populations that we see across the globe (Petzold & Magnan, 2019).

This depopulation disproportionately targets the most skilled and entrepreneurial elements of the younger workforce and, as a result, skilled, creative and innovative talent becomes less and less impactful in these regions. Without the development of entrepreneurial ecosystems, digital-creative education and support, young people will inevitably migrate to countries where aspirations are higher than the low-skill and low-wage service economy.

The creative 4IR, however, offers an opportunity to realign these economies away from an over-reliance on tourism and offers young people the chance to develop careers and opportunities in these digital, technology-based creative industries – a sector that is central to educational and economic aspiration and achievement. It also allows SIDS to be more attractive to inward investment and to retain more of the money that flows into the country through this trade. For example, leakage, the process by which revenue flows out of the host country to pay for imported products and services, is higher in the Maldives than almost anywhere else (UNCTAD, 2010).

The majority of resorts are owned by international brands and most of the food and drinks consumed at these resorts is produced outside the country. More than 80% of the indigenous workforce relies directly or indirectly on tourism. This financial dependence on a single industry leaves the Maldives vulnerable – as we've seen all too clearly recently. Salaries in the hospitality trade also tend to be low; work is often seasonal and with limited adherence to international labour standards (Ghosh et al., 2017).

The creative industries are however not something that are there to replace tourism, or the Blue Economy more widely. What they offer is the opportunity to develop broader economies and open up the development of digital-creative sectors that are powering global growth. They also enable the digital and creative transformation for these sectors, and indeed for many other parts of society and economy, particularly healthcare, education and government (Hearn et al., 2014).

So international agencies, finance providers and major corporations need to recognise that the impact of the 4IR on the creative industries means that the assumed importance of urban co-location no longer holds entirely true – that significant creative and cultural entrepreneurship need not be restricted to developed countries and major urban centres.

Kimura et al. (2019) talk about the impact of new technologies – 5G is particularly impactful here – and the lessening need for geographic proximity for producers, collaborative innovations and access to markets. The 5G trials and infrastructural developments happening now internationally have the ability to transform real-time collaboration, co-creation and creative content production. It is also the case that this technology is changing how we incubate, develop and manage creative clusters and ecosystems.

The evidence from the Platform Moving Image Cluster in the UK, discussed in the following chapter, shows that polycentric regions and peri-urban spaces can develop thriving and impactful digital-creative clusters if the right mechanisms, initiatives and leadership are put in place. By using technology and a greater understanding of the cluster ecosystems used in developing creative-digital economies, SIDS can ameliorate the negative impacts that geography, climate change, lack of human and natural resources and dispersed populations can have on innovation and entrepreneurialism.

Digital artefacts, technology solutions and creative content have no need of natural resource in their manufacture and are not limited by the usual distribution routes to market. Digital exports can become a significant revenue earner for these small states if strategies and policies can be put in place to create the education, skills and financial ecosystems to allow them to flourish.

The rise of these digital exports could see the digital-creative industries become the most important global sector for the twenty-first century, and it is crucial to understand that the 4IR is not just about robots taking jobs or AI helping us increase crop harvest. It is about fundamental shifts in what we think about manufacturing, trade and national economies. This then has significant impacts on how we sustainably develop the global creative economy as a whole, its inclusivity and its ability to offset some notable challenges.

The 4IR and the developing world

Research, development, discussion and practical implementation of the 4IR are largely focused on developed countries. Whilst these innovations are generally seen as universally positive, digital technology innovation also has the potential of creating increased inequality between nations and regions if new emerging, creative, knowledge-based sectors are not supported in developing regions.

The United Nations' International Labour Organisation has revealed that more than half of workers in Cambodia, Indonesia, Thailand, Vietnam and the Philippines, at least 137 million people, risk losing their jobs to automation in the next two decades (UNILO, 2018). The effect of automated production in South East Asia is predicted to be 'race to the bottom' as wages fall and worker rights and protections are stripped back.

Advanced manufacturing sees falling production costs and a lowering of the demand for labour in the process, thereby allowing companies to relocate their production back to the main home markets. The demand for humans then as part of even small-scale production is losing the comparative advantage to technology (Kazmer, 2014). In many of these production plants the labour requirement has fallen as much as 75% (World Economic Forum, 2018). Rather than requiring four workers in offshore plants, only one person is needed in planned onshore operations.

Whilst SIDS are not subject to the off-shoring of production by major corporations, the global shift in production, trade and employment presents real and significant challenges that impact on an increasingly volatile global market, only highlighted and exacerbated further by the 2020 Covid-19 pandemic. We saw what the impact of the financial crash of 2008 did to global luxury travel, and that has been dwarfed by the events of 2020. We must also not underestimate the effects on tourism of social and cultural upheaval caused by rising inequality coupled with social and political polarisation (Song & Lin, 2010).

All these factors play on the delicate nature of tourist decision-making. For many SIDS that rely primarily on tourism as the major employer and contributor to GDP, that increasing volatility is a major cause for concern. But the dire predictions around the negative impacts of the 4IR hide the positives that developing countries can derive from these new technologies of production and consumption. The new industries and opportunities of the 4IR can offset the impacts of that tourist market volatility.

For SIDS in particular, the 4IR could have a truly positive transformative effect, especially if we look at how these economies could join the creative industries revolution that has and continues to transform economies in the developed world.

The importance of 4IR to the SDGs

Technology and finance are seen as being the key factors in achieving the SDGs, finance allowing capital flows to implement projects on the ground and technology providing the tools, data and innovations to make it happen.

The 4IR is driven by the rapidly falling costs and increasing efficiency of digital technologies, allowing more people in more countries, especially now in the developing world, to access fast internet, smartphone technologies and mobile banking, for example. Whilst there are still many people in developing regions without access to these technologies, the ever cheaper costs associated with technology production are enabling that number to fall also. However, UNESCO's Director General, Audrey Azoulay, stressed an often ignored aspect of digital connectivity for poorer countries. She highlighted how the main factor preventing people in developing countries from using mobile internet is not affordability but poor literacy and digital skills (UNESCO, 2019). The challenge then in this instance is not technology but the governance, innovation and finance to make this happen.

One of the most positive actions that seeks to marry these technologies to creative innovators and entrepreneurs is the World Economic Forum's UpLink initiative, a new digital platform to crowdsource ideas and solutions to progressing the Global Goals. The World Economic Forum's report, *Unlocking Technology for the Global Goals* (World Economic Forum, 2020), makes the point that whilst the opportunities of the 4IR are undeniable, it is a case of using that technology to drive creative innovations that are married to social, environmental and cultural benefit, not just seeing technology application as the endpoint. These benefits also require considerable work to be done on data – both quality and access, the viability of new business models and policy environments and the vital importance of education, upskilling and reskilling.

Education and skills in the 4IR-enabled creative economy

The digital and technological transformation of the future labour market, and the resulting shifting demands placed on education and skills, is a major challenge for developing countries, as many tasks in agriculture, manufacturing and industrial production are being automated. This trend could result in widespread job losses if traditional employment sectors deploy more technology and education systems fail to adapt and open up alternative, knowledge-based, creative and innovation-based courses. South Africa, for example, is widely considered the African nation best prepared to succeed in the 4IR, yet according to the World Economic Forum, more than 40% of existing work activities in South Africa are susceptible to auto-mation. Although this is slightly lower than countries such as Nigeria, Kenya and Ethiopia, the impacts in South Africa may very well occur faster than in other sub-Saharan countries because of higher salary levels (WEF, 2018).

The pace of this change will require all workers to become active lifelong learners, developing and acquiring new skills on a continual basis. National gov-ernment education policy, along with higher education research and curricula development, has to recognise this shift and quickly adapt to mitigate the negative aspects of this economic and employment transformation.

The picture is even more acute in SIDS. Although these regions share many similarities to other developing countries, they also differ in some notable ones, making them an interesting case for seeing how education and skills training around 4IR technologies and business models can be implemented.

The often dispersed nature of island nations and regions means that education levels and competencies can be highly variable. The Maldives is an interesting case in point. Literacy levels are high, with over 90% of adolescent school leav-ers being bilingual in Dhiveni and English, school enrolment levels at over 96% and government-provided free education up to grade 12 (UNESCO, 2018). This enrolment drops sharply however post-secondary, with only one in five young people engaged in higher secondary education, due in large part to the majority of schools offering higher secondary education being located in the capital (World Bank, 2012).

The World Bank worked closely with the Maldives government under the Enhancing Education Development Project from 2013 to 2018 to address some of the challenges, with the Maldives government then embarking on a series of education reforms to develop a new curriculum. Whilst these reforms saw a new focus on education for the jobs market, its focus on technical and managerial skills aimed primarily at the tourism market meant that preparation for the rapidly changing global economic market was severely limited.

Whilst attracting more Maldivians into a local tourism jobs market that is domi-nated by expats seems logical, it doesn't speak to the aspirations of many young people for high-skill, high-pay, entrepreneurial opportunities.

In the economic recovery post-Covid-19, education and skills focused around the new industrial landscape of technology, innovation and creativity are essential. The development of critical, creative, problem-solving skills is seen as essential to the workforce of the 4IR, with the old notion of Science, Technology, Engi-neering and Maths (STEM) now looking a little outdated in its subject-specific focus. New forms of hybrid education are going to be required, for example, that involves the coupling of data science with cultural and critical theory, AI linking with languages, humanities and the wider liberal arts.

The interdisciplinary nature of many of the liberal arts degrees will become a central guiding principle for higher education, in particular in preparing graduates for the increasingly hyper-connected and cross-sector nature of 4IR economies (Penprase, 2018). For the Maldives then, and for all SIDS regions, education and skills have to step outside traditional norms.

Key technologies for creative island economies

The Information Technology Union released a report (ITU, 2019) on SIDS and ICT as part of the mid-term review of the SAMOA Pathway. It highlighted that there were some real positives but also challenges for SIDS in exploiting the opportunities that the growth in data speeds and internet accessibility opens up.

For the development of strong and sustainable creative economies in SIDS, access to technology is essential. Mobile broadband coverage has seen a significant increase since the 2014 Samoa conference, rising from 50% to 85% of the population. Mobile data costs have halved, and the majority of SIDS now have this data delivered through submarine fibre optic cables. So the challenge now is developing the education and skills to allow populations and island-based entrepreneurs to exploit this technology, along with the financial and regulatory environments to make the process of creative innovation as friction free as possible. Alongside this fast internet connectivity, there are some key 4IR technologies and opportunities for SIDS.

AI, ML and data

Central to any organisation, government or business today is timely, reliable and contextualised data, and the concept and usage of big data have become particularly widespread across many sectors. Although the description of big data is evolving, the understanding that it is made up of what Douglas (Douglas, 2001) describes as volume, velocity and variety is central. Added to that, Kitchin and McArdle (Kitchin & McArdle, 2016) describe characteristics of big data such as resolution, extensionality, relationality, indexicality and scalability.

Central to this use of big data are the tools of AI and ML. Data in and of itself has no value, it is only in the usage, contextualisation and application that data can impart value through insights into the dynamics of social, economic, cultural and natural systems. The volume of data produced has meant that AI and ML are central to how meaning can be derived though analytics.

For SIDS, data analytics can play a central role not only in the all-important Blue Economy, such as understanding changes in ocean ecosystems, fish stocks and trade flows, tourist spend, destination marketing and product development, but also in evidencing the impacts, opportunities and barriers of the knowledge economy. Key to all this however, and an issue for the use of AI and ML in data analytics, are the quality and contemporality of the data used to update and sharpen the ML algorithms and hence the quality and accuracy of the analytical process.

Data is a particular issue for the creative and cultural industries worldwide per se, and not just in relation to AI and ML applications. CCI data is highly variable in quality, dispersed across organisations and often outdated. This absence of data is particularly apparent in developing regions as a whole and notably in SIDS. Data for world trade in creative products and services is difficult to obtain because many developing countries do not track and report on the creative and cultural industries as an important sector. Assumptions and estimates therefore have to be made (UNCTAD, 2018).

There is an urgent need therefore for greater collaborative research, data aggregation and data analytics across all CCI sectors, with a particular emphasis on the developing world. Data is seen, quite rightly, as the crucial element of policy, strategic and commercial decision-making. Yet the assumption that we just need data to make the right decisions is flawed. Data only becomes useful through its interpretation, and interpretation is governed by culture – in its widest sense. The amount of data is also increasing exponentially, making it harder and harder to make decisions based on clear understandings and interpretations.

Decision-making becomes vastly more difficult as you increase the amount of information surrounding that decision, and the number of ways to get something wrong, certainly in strategy, decision-making and policy implementation, always significantly outnumbers the number of ways to get it right. The impact of data on the development of sustainable economies in SIDS, particularly those essential knowledge-based sectors, will rely on the wider research and development community to put in place the mechanisms and understanding to draw pertinent analyses from the rapidly expanding mass of data.

Blockchain and cryptocurrencies

Despite its popular perception, blockchain is far more than just a tool for cryptocurrency transactions. It is a new global infrastructure that can transform commercial, societal and governmental processes and address many key challenges. For SIDS, the adoption of blockchain technologies can work in a number of ways.

Many SIDS have strong cultural heritage assets, both tangible and intangible, and the ability to monetise this, not just as a tourist attraction but as a valuable international goods export sector, can be significant. For example, allowing cultural and creative designer-makers to connect with clients, track and monetise their products more successfully.

Blockchain enables these designer-makers to build a comprehensive historical record of their goods that creates a more secure and efficient supply chain management process. This ability to track the creation, export, distribution and purchase of an individual cultural asset allows consumers to trust the source and integrity of any particular asset (Yaga et al., 2018). It can also impact the vital tourist sector, enabling Fintech innovations such as the blockchain platform in

Aruba that allows local companies to connect directly with tourists and reclaim loss revenues from the monopoly of foreign agencies (Travers, 2017).

The Caribbean Tourism Organisation is also promoting crypto-payment to boost the local and regional tourist industry (Callahan, 2018). The Eastern Caribbean Central Bank (ECCB) has been working on a regional cryptocurrency, a digital version of the Eastern Caribbean Dollar (ECD), called the DXCD. The original ECD is the legal tender of eight regional island countries: Anguilla, Antigua and Barbuda, the Commonwealth of Dominica, Grenada, Montserrat, St Kitts and Nevis, St Lucia and St Vincent and the Grenadines. The ECCB has served as the monetary authority of these islands since 1983 and is a successful example of fiscal cooperation in the region. It is targeting 2025 as a date for seeing a 50% reduction in the use of cash, an 80% reduction in the use of cheques and a growth of between 40% and 60% in the use of credit cards, debit cards and electronic payment systems (ECCB, 2017).

The challenges of monetary union across small island states though is clear, with physical currency transfer an obvious barrier whilst, despite the ECCB governance, banking transfer and facilities are not as unified or fluidly implemented as they could be. The case for the digital currency then becomes compelling in this instance. The removal of frictions and inefficiencies it is hoped will help drive economic growth in the recovery from Covid-19.

As is common in many SIDS regions with dispersed populations, especially outside capital cities, a large proportion of the population are underbanked, often put off by the sometimes large fees to transfer monies between islands. Such digital currencies then offer the ability for low-cost, fast and flexible transfer of funds via smartphone, not just between private individuals, but in B2B and B2C transactions. This secure digital transfer of funds, coupled with the ability of blockchain to track and verify creative and cultural goods from local designer-makers could see a significant growth in creative micro-business start-ups and exports.

Immersive technologies

Much is talked about the revolution that virtual reality and augmented reality (AR) will have on the creative and entertainment industries. The ability to break out of the two-dimensional storytelling paradigm that we've had for more than 100 years opens up some ground-breaking possibilities for content creators across economic sectors (Corallo et al., 2019).

However, as highlighted in the other chapters of this book, the discussion around technology implementation and the resultant changing business models of distribution and monetisation remain stubbornly siloed. The central pillar of the impact of immersive technologies on the creative and cultural sector is their combination and collaboration with other sectors.

We see creative content producers and technology specialists developing innovative products and applications in sectors such as architecture, healthcare, tourism and construction. Whilst immersive technology will impact the entertainment industries, in particular the gaming industry, it is how these technologies drive cross-sector collaborations that is most exciting.

For instance, animators and visual effects artists are working with immersive technology companies to create virtual new building walk-throughs for clients, using the skills of texture mapping and lighting to produce highly lifelike and therefore more instructive models for clients (Paes et al., 2017). In similar ways, 3D artists are working with digital health companies and national organisations to enable the visualisation of virtual operations as part of training and diagnostic procedures. All of these examples see the creative sector collaborating, innovating and becoming an essential part of the economic fabric of nations and regions.

Creative immersive content and tourism

With tourism playing such a significant role in the economic fabric of many SIDS, the growth of creative content, delivered through augmented, merged and virtual realities, presents a significant opportunity to enhance visitor experiences, engage new audiences in tourist destinations and increase the marketing reach and penetration of place-specific attractions. Mura et al. suggest that virtual digital worlds are becoming central to the success of the tourism industry (Mura et al., 2017).

There have already been numerous uses of AR technology to enhance visitor experiences by overlaying educational or experiential content onto real scenes (Jung et al., 2016) and used particularly in heritage tourism, where immersive technology applications have engaged with places, artefacts and events.

An example of this is the 5G Smart Tourism project in the UK city of Bath that successfully completed the first public trial of a smartphone AR application at the historic Roman Baths in December 2018. Over 100 visitors experienced reconstructions of the Baths at key moments in history on a mobile AR app. High-quality 360-degree video was streamed over the project's network, which included the first UK deployment of a 60 GHz mesh network. The project partnered with Oscar-winning animation company Aardman to model the historical aspects of the Baths for visitors (Wilson, 2019).

These technologies can have a significant impact on destination marketing, allowing tourist boards and resort owners to engage with potential clients on a far deeper and more personal way. The impacts on competition for tourism revenue look only set to increase in the post-Covid-19 recovery, thereby increasing the need for countries and resorts to find any competitive advantage they can and to market directly and impactfully to potential clients.

The encouragement of domestic tourism, due to the ongoing restrictions to outward travel, will largely not be applicable to SIDS regions, given the often small domestic market and low- to middle-income nature of many of the countries (UN ESCAP, 2020).

So for SIDS, the promise of a gradual return of foreign exchange revenue as tourism recovers must be seen in the light of growing competition for that revenue. It will necessitate new technologies in destination marketing, along with technology-enhanced experiences in these locations, hotels and resorts and the lessons of how major urban tourist destinations have used the 'smart city' concept could hold some valuable lessons for SIDS regions.

Smart cities and smart islands

Much of the discussion of the role of smart cities has focused on large countries and major cities. However, smart city approaches have real relevance to small island states as the previous examples show and not just in terms of the usual specific 4IR technology developments. They can instigate a broader, connected innovation approach that cannot just improve city-wide facilities management but also foster human resource development through training and skills access, help micro and small businesses access finance and markets, as we've seen with blockchain, and improve social and cultural structures.

The concept of 'smartness' was developed during debates on urban politics in the United States at the start of the 1990s and is linked to the concept of smart growth that was coined by the New Urbanism movement (Downs, 2005). This was taken on in 2008, when IBM began work on a 'smarter cities' concept as part of its Smarter Planet initiative.

The concept of a smart city is based around the idea of making large urban centres more environmentally sustainable, with its main goal being reducing greenhouse gas emissions through the use of new technologies (Russo et al., 2014). Most smart city definitions focus on the use of 4IR technologies such as AI-enabled data analysis and the internet of things to impact transport systems, green energy systems and logistics. This can also broaden out into other definitions that link these technologies to better quality of life and decreased environmental impacts (Lombardi, 2011).

There is also though an important human role in the technological development and success of smart cities, one that can have a significant impact on the economic and environmental sustainability of urban centres (Nam & Pardo, 2011). Angelidou (2014) also discusses this, seeing then that both technology- and human-centred approaches are vital to smart city success.

This perhaps would align more closely with the UN Sustainable Development Goal of "inclusive, safe, resilient and sustainable cities". This urban SDG has ten targets and 14 indicators, and whilst the concept of 'smart cities' is not mentioned in these statements, the UN's Partnership Platform details the establishment of the United Smart Cities programme, a project jointly initiated by the United Nations Economic Commission for Europe, the Organisation for International Relations and Industrial Partners.

An example of how smart city thinking can be used in small island states can be seen in the new city of Hulhumalé in the Maldives. Located three kilometres from the capital Malé, it is currently under development and will be founded on full-fibre connectivity, giving the new city Asia's first gigabit-enabled Open Access Network. The goal is to push forward the digitalisation of government services, businesses and lifestyles and drive economic evolution as part of a drive to create a smart, modern city. The smart city solutions aim to implement smart traffic management systems and utility grids and to enhance community engagement through the development of a Geographical Information System (GIS).

This new development not only allows the usual smart city benefits but will enable greater uptake and implementation of the tourist user experience – though more location-based, immersive and augmented experiences – along with the creative and knowledge-based innovation opportunities of 5G-enabled production and distribution.

Whilst this development sits very much with the technology-driven, smart city concept, the opportunities for replicability, albeit on a smaller scale, for outlying atolls could see these smart city benefits positively impacting the social, cultural and economic life of the country's dispersed populations.

For these regions, and many similar SIDS populations, remodelling the smart city concept along the human, social and cultural axis, whilst keeping the underlying digital technology infrastructure benefits, offers a means of seeing smart city concepts benefitting small island states. Whilst this idea of 'smart island' has been discussed before (see Chamberlain et al., 2013, Desogus et al., 2019), much of the work retains the 'smart' focus from previous city-based technology developments.

For SIDS then, a redefinition of the concept and understanding of 'smart' is perhaps required, moving beyond the 'governance through technology' approach to a more holistic, human-centred and innovation-based understanding. This could be conceived as moving from a 'smart island' concept to that of a 'creative island'.

Smart cities become creative islands

So there are some key lessons here then for the sustainable development of small islands as creative islands, particularly when we look at how knowledge-based, creative and cultural sectors can improve resilience. The implementation of technology in these islands will not be the same as in cities, given the often dispersed and polycentric nature of SIDS.

Developing a concept for smart island development should therefore encompass not just a focus on technology deployment and implementation but an integration of the development of education, knowledge-based creative innovation, entrepreneurial ecosystems and governance within a human-centred framework driven to deliver social, economic and environmental benefits.

This description deliberately goes beyond the normal smart city or smart island narrative to encompass ideas of smart as creative, knowledge-based social and cultural structures. Smart in this instance then brings technology, human-centred creative innovation and sustainable development together to create a more rounded and cogent form of the term.

The most important aspect of smart island development is in improving the lives of its citizens by building resilience and sustainable, inclusive growth. Technology is a valuable tool here but is not the end in itself. The solution is to integrate the implementation of SDGs, aligned to digital-creative innovation and enabled by the use of industry 4.0 technologies. Smart islands then become more than just the transplanting of smart city ideas of the governance of people, traffic and energy flows through IoT technologies and big data. Smart islands in this concept then become creative islands, an idea based around the human meaning of the term.

Conclusion

The creation of technology-enabled, but human-centred open innovation ecosystems, focused on creative knowledge–based sustainable economic development presents an opportunity for SIDS that has had little discussion up to this point. Whilst these technologies have seen localised reports on applications for specific sectors in these regions, namely around tourism, the appreciation of the broader transformative aspects still require research and strategic direction. The ability to drive private sector investment will be crucial in order to create the entrepreneurial and innovation landscape that this transformation will require, but this has to be done in conjunction with the delivery of greater education and skills around the creative, social and cultural impacts and uses.

This will allow island governments and communities to not only connect with the new global trade systems created by this technology but also deliver real, on-the-ground applications and impacts. If these elements can be implemented to support 4IR transformation for SIDS, then it can go a considerable way to ameliorating the vulnerabilities we discussed in the opening chapter.

References

Angelidou, M. 2014. Smart City Policies: A Spatial Approach. *Cities*, 41, pp. S3–S11.

Bandura, R., et al. 2019. Beyond Technology the Fourth Industrial Revolution in the Developing World. A Report of the CSIS Project on Prosperity and Development, Centre for Strategic and International Studies.

Callahan, M.A. 2018. The Rise of Cryptocurrency in the Caribbean. Accessed at www.caribbeannewsnow.com.

Chamberlain, A., Malizia, A. & Dix, A.J. 2013. Engaging in Island Life: Big Data, Micro Data, Domestic Analytics and Smart Islands. Proceedings of the 2013 ACM Conference on Pervasive and Ubiquitous Computing Adjunct Publication, pp. 721–724. Association for Computing Machinery, New York.

Corallo, A., Marra, M. & Pascarelli, C. 2019. Transmedia Digital Storytelling for Cultural Heritage Visiting Enhanced Experience. In De Paolis, L. & Bourdot, P. (Eds.), *Augmented Reality, Virtual Reality and Computer Graphics. AVR 2019 vol 11614*. Springer, New York.

Department of Culture Media and Sport. 2020. *DCMS Sectors Economic Estimates 2018: GVA*. DCMS, London.

Desogus, G., Mistretta, P. & Garau, C. 2019. Smart Islands: A Systematic Review on Urban Policies and Smart Governance. In *International Conference on Computational Science and its Applications*, pp. 137–151. Springer, Cham.

Douglas, L. 2001. *3D Data Management: Controlling Volume, Velocity and Variety. Application Delivery Strategies, February 2001, File 949*. Meta Group, Stamford.

Downs, A. 2005. Smart Growth: Why We Discuss It More Than We Do it. *Journal of the American Planning Association*, 71(4), pp. 367–378.

Eastern Caribbean Central Bank. 2017. ECCB Strategic Plan 2017–2021. St. Kitts and Nevis. Accessed at www.eccb-centralbank.org/p/strategic-plan-2017-2021.

Financial Times. 2019. Apple Worth More than US Stock Index's Energy Sector. Accessed January 18, 2020 at www.ft.com/content/4a8ab20a-1149-11ea-a7e6-62bf4f9e548a.

Fortune 500. 2019. Fortune Magazine. Accessed at http://fortune.com/fortune500.

Ghosh, R.N., Siddique, M.A.B. & Gabbay, R. 2017. International Tourism and Economic Development. In *Tourism and Economic Development* (pp. 19–29). Routledge, London.

Hearn, G., Bridgstock, R., Goldsmith, B. & Rodgers, J. (Eds.). 2014. *Creative Work Beyond the Creative Industries: Innovation, Employment and Education*. Elgar Publications, Cheltenham.

International Telecommunications Union. 2019. *Small Island Developing States and ICTs: Mid-Term Review of the SAMOA Pathway*. ITU Publications, Thematic Reports, Geneva.

Jung, T.H., tom Dieck, M.C., Lee, H. & Chung, N. 2016. Effects of Virtual Reality and Augmented Reality on Visitor Experiences in Museum. In Inversini, A. & Schegg, R (Eds.), *Information and Communication Technologies in Tourism*, pp. 621–635. Springer, New York.

Kamal, M. & Diksha, D. 2019. Investigating ICT's for Education in Marginalised Communities. MWAIS 2019 Proceedings 17.

Kazmer, D. 2014. Manufacturing Outsourcing, Onshoring, and Global Equilibrium. Business Horizons.57.10.

Kimura, F., Shrestha, R. & Narjoko, D. 2019. The Digital and Fourth Industrial Revolution and ASEAN Economic Transformation. In Kimuar, F., Anbomozhi, V. & Nishimura, H. (Eds.), *Transforming and Deepening the ASEAN Community*, pp. 1–23. ERIA, Jakarta.

Kitchin, R. & McArdle, G. 2016. What Makes Big Data, Big Data? Exploring the Ontological Characteristics of 26 Datasets. *Big Data and Society*, 3(1), pp. 2053951716631130.

Ling-yee, L. & Ogunmokun, G. 2015. Determinants of Export Performance: Research Evidence from Mainland China. In *Global Perspectives in Marketing for the 21st Century*, pp. 166–166.

Lombardi, P. 2011. New Challenges in the Evaluation of Smart Cities. *Network Industries Quarterly*, 13(3), pp. 8–10.

Malkawi, B.H., 2019. Digitalization of International Trade. *Journal and Law and Technology*, 23.

Mpofu, R. & Nicolaides, A. 2019. Frankenstein and the Fourth Industrial Revolution(4IR): Ethics and Human Rights Considerations. *African Journal of Hospitality, Tourism and Leisure*, 8(5).

Mura, P., Tavakoli, R. & Sharif, S.P. 2017. Authentic but Not Too Much: Exploring Perceptions of Authenticity of Virtual Tourism. *Information technology and Tourism*, 17(2), pp. 1–15.

Nam, T. & Pardo, T.A. 2011. Conceptualising Smart City with Dimensions of Technology, People and Institutions. Proceedings of the 12th Annual International Digital Government Research Conference: Digital Government Innovation in Challenging Times, pp. 282–291.

Nawaz, S.J., Sharma, K., Wyne, S., Patwary, M.N. & Asaduzzaman, M. 2019. Quantum Machine Learning for 6G Communications Networks: State-of-the-art and Vision for the Future. *IEEE Access*, 7, pp. 46317–46350.

OECD. 2019. Trade Policy Brief on Digital Trade. Accessed at www.oecd.org/trade/topics/digital-trade.

Paes, D., Arantes, E. & Irizarry, J. 2017. Immersive Environment for Improving the Understanding of Architectural 3D Models: Comparing User Spatial Perception between Immersive and Traditional Virtual Reality Systems. *Automation in Construction*, 84, pp. 292–303.

Penprase, B.E. 2018. The Fourth Industrial Revolution and Higher Education. In Gleason, N. (Ed.), *Higher Education in the Era of the Fourth Industrial Revolution*. Palgrave Macmillan, London.

Petzold, J. & Magnan, A.K., 2019. Climate Change: Thinking Small Islands Beyond Small Island Developing States (SIDS). *Climatic Change*, 152(1), pp. 145–165.

Russo, F., Rindone, C. & Panuccio, P. 2014. The Process of Smart City Definition at an EU Level. *WIT Transactions on Ecology and the Environment*, 191, pp. 979–989.

Song, H. & Lin, S. 2010. Impacts of the Financial and Economic Crisis on Tourism in Asia. *Journal of Travel Research*, 49(1), 16–30.

Travers, J. 2017. *Can Ethereum's Blockchain Help Aruba Reclaim Its Travel Industry?* BTC Manager. Accessed at www.btcmanager.com.

UN ESCAP. 2020. The Future of Tourism Post COVID-19. Accessed at www.unescap.org/blob/future-tourism-post-covid-19.

UNCTAD. 2010. *The Least Developed Countries Report 2010: Towards a New International Development Architecture for LDCs*. UNCTAD, Geneva.

UNCTAD. 2018. *Creative Economy Outlook: Trends in International Trade in Creative Industries*. UNCTAD, Geneva.

UNCTAD. 2019. *Proceedings of Trade and Development Board*. UNCTAD, Geneva, 2nd session, 3–7 May 2010.

UNESCO. 2018. *Children in Maldives: Analysis of Children of the Maldives from Census 2014*. UNESCO, Paris.

UNESCO. 2019. *I'd Blush if I Could: Closing Gender Divides in Digital Skills Through Education*. UNESCO, Paris.

UNILO. 2018. Research Department Working Paper No. 36. Robots Worldwide: The Impact of Automation on Employment and Trade.

Wilson, P. 2019. State of Smart Cities in UK and beyond. *IET Smart Cities*, 1(1), pp. 19–22.

World Bank. 2012. *Enhancing the Quality of Education in the Maldives: Challenges and Prospects*. South Asian Human Development Sector Report No. 51. World Bank, Washington, DC.

World Economic Forum. 2018. *Future of Jobs Report*. WEF, Geneva. Accessed at www.weforum.org/reports/the-future-of-jobs-report-2018.

World Economic Forum. 2020. *Unlocking Technology for the Global Goals*. WEF, Geneva. Accessed at www.weforum.org/reports/unlocking-technology-for-the-global-goals.

Yaga, D., Mell, P., Roby, N. & Scarfone, K. 2018. *Blockchain Technology Overview*. NIST, US Department of Commerce Publications, Washington, DC.

4 Clusters beyond the city – a decentralised model

Introduction

We saw in the last chapter how the technologies of the 4IR could have a transforming effect on SIDS and how these technologies could be transferred from the 'smart city' to the 'smart island', and, in doing so, reconceptualise these terminologies for SIDS to become 'creative islands'. The smart city however is not the only development concept that can, with some innovative thinking, be transferred and transformed from the big city to the small island.

One of the most dominant narratives around economic growth, regional development and urban regeneration has been the concept of clusters. They have become a well-defined method of growing and supporting an industrial sector and a popular policy tool for city and regional governments looking to put in place strategies and actions to deliver that growth.

In the digital-creative and cultural industries in particular, clusters have long been recognised as a method of enhancing and sustaining a strong creative ecosystem, making a statement that a cluster is being, or has been, established in a region and putting a flag in the ground that there is something worthy of attention in this space. This is particularly valuable for regions with economic, social or infrastructural challenges.

When we think of the challenges faced by island states, their economic restrictions and vulnerabilities and the need for broadening their economic bases out from the Blue Economy to a knowledge-based, digital-creative economy, can clusters play a role there?

Given their small-scale, often dispersed populations across archipelagic geographies, and limited domestic economies, establishing and maintaining a successful economic cluster may seem problematic. Whilst the growth and performance of digital technologies can be a significant tool in making this happen, the global economy is also being rapidly reshaped by technological innovation and its impact on trade and business models.

Although the growth of global digital exports and the resulting huge expansion of the creative industries is an enormous opportunity for small island states and developing economies more widely, this digital-creative transformation has also seen the rise of a winner-takes-all spatio-economic dynamic.

The concentration of creative-digital-technology companies in major cities in developed regions has meant that growth and opportunity is becoming more and more concentrated.

The worry for many regional leaders, development organisations and smaller countries, particularly island nations, is that they are increasingly being left behind by this change. Whilst creative clusters offer mechanisms for brining key actors together to offset some of these challenges, along with the creative hubs so often regarded as central to the establishment of such clusters, they have always been seen as native to large urban centres.

Certainly, clusters in small island states would, if the traditional model were to be applied, face some significant and perhaps insurmountable problems. But does this still have to be the case?

If clusters are to play a role in developing creative and cultural industries in SIDS, then the understanding of the structure and role of cluster initiatives needs to be revisited. If we are to prevent not just small island states but rural communities, towns and dispersed populations in developed as well as developing countries from effectively being shut out of this economic growth, then cluster initiatives have to find new ways of working beyond the city.

The ubiquity of clusters

The popularity of clusters stems from the idea that cluster initiatives offer a vehicle for driving and managing the complex set of stakeholder relationships and targeted investments needed to address the growth constraints of a local or regional sector. City regions in particular see investment in creative industries clusters as a method of regeneration, often as a move from traditional industries to a more digital-creative, innovation-based economy.

Pittsburgh is a good example of this, the city government setting out a clear strategy of investing in and supporting a transition from a struggling former steel town, one of the classic 'Rust Belt' cities, to a centre for creative and technology innovations. The impact of the Pittsburgh Technology Council and the Createch Festival shows just how valuable investments in establishing networks and clusters can be.

The success of clusters has been based on the idea that the gradual coming together of firms in a similar sector starts to generate greater innovation, ideas exchange, collaboration and skills development. This critical mass of people, skills and knowledge then starts to reinforce itself through the establishment of new start-up companies, greater inward investment and the eventual development of a cluster 'brand'.

The best-known examples of this are the film and TV sector in Hollywood and the technology sector of Silicon Valley. Hollywood has been the global centre for film production since the early 1900s, and despite the growth of strong production centres in countries like the UK and India, the entertainment cluster in Los Angeles has retained its pre-eminence. Initially drawn to California by the clear skies, long hours of daylight for shooting and the quality and multitude of different landscapes, Hollywood eventually became a cluster of hugely powerful companies that have dominated the entertainment landscape for a century.

Silicon Valley grew out of the innovations and start-ups generated by graduates of universities like Stanford. This small group of technology businesses attracted talent and other related companies until it grew into a cluster of global significance.

Such is the strength of the Silicon Valley brand that the term has become part of the lexicon for regional technology development. The burgeoning digital cluster in Santa Monica in California has called itself Silicon Beach, and the computer games cluster in Leamington Spa in England has used the term Silicon Spa to brand itself and lay down a marker for the region.

Both Hollywood and Silicon Valley followed a process of organic growth and development, but as we've discussed with the success of Pittsburgh, clusters can often be created through the formal acknowledgement and naming of even a small agglomeration of companies by a local or regional government or development agency, allied to a long-term strategic goal, associated resource inputs and committed, expert leadership.

Clusters and cluster initiatives

So in discussing the development, roles and impacts of creative clusters, it is important to note here the difference between a cluster and a cluster initiative. Whilst the former refers to the concept that describes the real economic phenomenon of concentrations of specific sector activities such as Silicon Valley or Hollywood, the latter describes an initiative or political effort to create, maintain or upgrade an economic stronghold or cluster (Ketels et al., 2006).

These cluster initiatives can help an emerging cluster to become established and then reach much higher levels of performance, for example by strengthening linkages or facilitating collective action to improve the cluster-specific business environment (Porter & Stern, 2001). These cluster initiatives or programmes are usually seen to take on a variety of roles or strategic priorities that vary from regional to national activities.

The most common are cluster programmes that focus on regional economic development through the support of a particular industry sector. The aim is to make the cluster internationally competitive whilst using this profile to further build the cluster brand and regional recognition. These clusters are typically city-based and feed into the 'place marketing' or 'place branding' ambitions of the city council or government.

This type of regional cluster initiative can then lead into programmes that focus on the development of national industries, ones that are seen as being of national strategic importance, such as the creative and cultural industries in the UK. This type of cluster initiative seeks to build on the already developed and successful regional innovation with programmes that go beyond the regional dimension by promoting national and international collaboration with other clusters (European Creative and Cultural Industries Alliance, 2012).

Alongside cluster initiatives based around industry sectors there are also those that are centred on research bases that focus on the commercial exploitation of the R&D. This can be regional, such as those based around major universities, or national, again with research sectors that are seen to have national strategic importance. This research focus can then become the centre of an industry cluster as start-ups are launched based on this R&D and a network created that may form the nucleus of a cluster (Federal Ministry of Economics and Technology, Germany, 2009).

These traditional models of cluster initiatives are based on a number of key traits and have formed the bedrock strategy for national-, regional- and city-based cluster development. Many of these key points will hold true as cluster development changes and adapts to the changing environment spoken about previously, but there are some notable areas where concepts need to change.

Key to the success of all these cluster initiatives has been the axis of industry–government–education, often referred to as the Triple Helix. Whilst clusters generally need to be industry led in order that the sector feels that the initiative is a ground-up collaboration and not a top-down exercise, public investment by national, regional and city governments are needed to catalyse the cluster, give it stability and provide the resources for the cluster to act in support of its industry members. Universities then support this process through education and research, feeding the skills and talent that will fuel the growth of the cluster.

This Triple Helix, though, has to form the basis of a complete ecosystem, one that is regenerative, sustainable and competitive. So clusters, despite the various points of focus mentioned previously, cannot sit apart from the key stakeholders, political institutions and processes and wider supply chains. This also has to be matched to committed and passionate leadership, typically a senior figure within the regional sector. Often driven in part by a social, philanthropic purpose, these leaders are crucial to bringing together the rest of the sector, the political and education leaders in the region and the wider stakeholders, such as chambers of commerce, regional development agencies, investors and financial institutions.

If cluster development initiatives are to have real impact, particularly in challenging regions, then strategies have to reflect the changing face of trade, economic growth and the local and regional needs of emerging sectors rather than being preoccupied with the interests of large companies and established sectors with a stronghold in the region. This can be seen as particularly true with small island states and the unwavering focus on the Blue Economy – to the exclusion of other sectors such as the digital-creative industries.

Identifying and establishing clusters

This approach is also reinforced by the use of often over-generalised data systems to identify which emerging clusters have the potential for growth and which should therefore be supported. Whilst this initially seems like a sensible approach to cluster identification, the systems of analysis are often flawed.

This identification is typically initially done through an analysis of employment, production output and numbers of companies. This is driven by the use of industry classification codes such as SIC in the UK and NAICS in the United States, Canada and Mexico.

The issue with using these codes as a baseline for decision-making is their inflexible and hierarchical nature. Clusters are complex, cross-sector, multi-dimensional, dynamic systems that extend both vertically and horizontally. Using these codes as a method of cluster identification runs the risk of either missing an emerging cluster, because the particular sector has a narrow codification but far reaching cross-sector supply and distribution chains, or overestimating the size of a cluster because these codes do not necessarily relate to each other in reality.

Another system that has been used extensively in cluster analysis but is equally problematic is the Location Quotient (LQ) method. This is a way of quantifying how concentrated an industry is within a particular area when compared to the country or region as a whole. For example, if animation studios in a city or region account for 2% of jobs but only 1% of jobs nationally, then the region's animation companies have an LQ of 2, which means that this region has double the concentration of animation studios than is the typical.

Whilst this may seem to offer a useable, measurable approach to analysing clusters, an important problem with the LQ system is that there is no quantifiable approach to what constitutes a significant cluster. There is also a lack of contextualisation in this method.

A local industry may have a low LQ but have considerable growth potential because the market for its products are large and vice versa. The digital-creative industries are a particularly good example for this. Highly successful, internationally renowned companies can have a global market but exist in groups of small or even micro companies that are highly interconnected and interdependent. The opposite of that can also be misleading in that a high LQ can be the result of a single large company, thereby not being a cluster at all.

Decisions around cluster development and investment then need to find a more suitable method to assess the complexity and dynamism of regional sectors. The blunt instruments of industry classification codes and LQ analysis have proved to be ineffective. This is partly due to a lack of data and contextual analysis in the creative and cultural industries, and this has to be addressed if smarter, more strategic and more focused public investments are to be made in cluster development.

This is hugely important as that initial public investment, allied to data that is properly contextualised, can then leverage more private and public initiative and investment. This must be at the forefront of any jobs, growth and investment agenda. In order for policy in this area to achieve its impact, priorities need to be set according to the geographical and thematic context of the investment.

Clusters and hubs

This leads onto the second point of difference from traditional clusters that is important to recognise, particularly for SIDS and their physical and geographical structures.

Most cluster initiatives are anchored around a physical centre or hub. It is often seen as essential proof that the city or region is serious about the development of the particular sector. Considerable resource has been put into the creation of spaces where entrepreneurs, start-ups, researchers and creatives can come together to facilitate innovation, collaboration and knowledge spillovers. The thinking behind this is that whilst firms, facilities and activities may be dispersed across a city region, the hub provides a focus for all the positive action noted earlier.

This focus on the importance of hubs to successful clusters links closely to the argument around why 'place' is important for creative and cultural industries (Comunian et al., 2010). This argument sits upon two main pillars. First, the creative economy is primarily based upon the knowledge, talent and innovation of creative individuals and companies, which can be seen as a point of difference between the CCIs and other industrial manufacturing sectors that are often relocated to parts of the world where labour costs are generally lower.

Second, the success of the creative industries is seen as being tightly linked to the social and cultural fabric of a city or city region. Place therefore has an impact on the nature of the creative economy in which it is situated. The creative hub then becomes an identifiable and physical manifestation of the nature of the 'place', not only an important factor in driving collaborative innovation but also part of the outward facing 'brand' of the cluster and the city (Ferilli et al., 2012).

The ability of creative entrepreneurs to repurpose existing, old or run-down buildings in the centre of declining post-industrial cities has become something of a cliché but has seen the regeneration of many of these cities across the globe. This led to city governments seeing the impact of these creative sectors on the physical and social repurposing of old buildings as a way of revitalising these troubled city precincts. Hubs became part of regeneration plans, economic strategies and social interventions and have without a doubt been a huge success story in the rise of the creative and cultural sectors as a force for economic, cultural and social good.

Whilst all this may be true, the perception that clusters can primarily only work with a physical hub, and that the hub is located in a major city, has seen the approach and thinking around clusters remain rather one-dimensional. There has to be a shift in thinking around creative cluster development that recognises that funding yet another 'creative hub' in a major Western capital city is simply not an investment with a strong-enough return.

Whilst the report on creative clusters by NESTA (Chapain et al., 2010) follows much of this traditional thinking, there is a key piece of analysis in that report that, despite now being ten years old, points to a crucial aspect of twenty-first-century cluster development and the role of creative hubs.

The report talks of the importance of connectivity between the various actors and participants in a local or regional creative economy. In today's hyper-connected world therefore, the 'layers of connectivity' in a creative cluster can take many forms and be facilitated in many ways. As we've seen during the Covid-19 pandemic in 2020, that connectivity is becoming not only increasingly important but also increasingly virtual. Whilst many may see this as a way forward and something that can be especially applicable to SIDS, the concept of a physical meeting place is still important, so simply making every hub virtual is not the answer.

The social connectivity between creative and cultural practitioners and innovators is an essential part of this economy, so 'real world' hubs remain a vital element of how creative economies can grow and how entrepreneurs in these sectors can connect and flourish. It is how these hubs are conceptualised and they then respond to and strengthen those layers of connectivity that, especially in the case of SIDS, need to be reworked.

Clusters and hubs in 'other' geographies

Clusters, and creative clusters in particular, tend to be associated with larger metropolitan areas, mainly because the creative workforce are seen as being young and dynamic, needing an equally thriving and dynamic cultural and social scene in which to flourish. The argument for the linking of cluster development and success to the cities agenda is that capital and other leading cities are in a better position to reap agglomeration economies, attract knowledge-intensive service activities and exploit the increased use of information and communications technology (Leunig & Overman, 2008).

However, many capital and tier-two cities are starting to see the negative impacts of traffic congestion, the high cost of land, increasingly fractured and marginalised populations within these cities and infrastructural deterioration. These factors are leading to marginal returns, which make them less competitive and not necessarily able to provide the best return on investment (Dijkstra et al., 2013).

In this instance the development of smaller cities and towns offer the possibility of strong secondary and tertiary growth centres that can then deliver a more even, polycentric and inclusive development. The importance of regional growth in the UK for instance, in particular regions outside London and the South East, has been highlighted by successive governments, and clusters provide the mechanisms whereby this can be targeted and accelerated (Bakshi & Mateos-Garcia, 2016).

It is important to realise however that clusters in towns and smaller cities cannot be developed using the same structures and benchmarks as those in major cities. This holds especially true for SIDS, with their particular challenges and geographical traits. These locations are often seen as problematic from the point of view of cluster development, so it is important that growth policies, at both regional and national levels, do not simply 'pick winners'. It is without doubt easier to develop and see superficial benefits from developing and supporting creative clusters in larger, growing cities, but it is in towns and smaller cities where cluster initiatives are actually most valuable and can have the most impact in terms of a more even development (European Creative and Cultural Industries Alliance, 2014).

Creative industries and place

The connection between the creative industries and place has been well documented theoretically (Oksanen & Stahle, 2013), as creativity and innovation are typically associated with both a region and a competitive advantage (Lazzaretti et al., 2009). City or regional governments then look to build this competitive advantage by defining their regional growth strategies around the identification and support of creative clusters, creative quarters and creative hubs (Foord, 2009).

Creative industry clusters however are not solely formed through urbanisation economies. Creative production and innovation rely on a number of other important factors, such as collective learning, access to a knowledge base and to global networks (Lazzaretti et al., 2009; Chapain & Comunian, 2010).

The priority given to cities as centres of creative industries also tends to focus on elements such as quality of life, social diversity and cultural infrastructure as being essential to creative economy success (Kong, 2012). This integration of clustering factors means that although the sector is constituted mainly of SMEs or even micro companies, along with a large and highly mobile freelance workforce, creative clusters are active in shaping regional and/or local culture-oriented strategies as part of a generative or regenerative activity.

The scale and scope of creative clusters though can be highly variable, so it is important not to dismiss creative communities, companies and emerging clusters in smaller cities, towns and connecting rural spaces, in what Cole (2008) terms 'the other geographies' of creative production.

These 'other geographies' however are typically relegated behind larger metropolitan areas – the primary focus of the majority of creative cluster research and development. So, whilst Fundeanu and Badele (2014) argue that clusters have reached a "quasi-paradigmatic" status in regional development thinking due to government policies that support the establishment and development of clusters as catalysts of growth and innovation (Hermans et al., 2010), for creative clusters outside larger cities, that government support and crucially, the role in regional growth strategy development, particularly in regions where traditional industries play a dominant role, is not always evident.

Analysis from NESTA (Mateos-Garcia et al., 2018) suggests that those places with strong creative economies see those strengths spread into other industries, potentially making them more innovative and productive, yet analysis on this scale tends to use location quotient data that, as we've seen, often misses the particular circumstances of clusters in towns and smaller cities.

This is an important lesson for national industrial strategies and agencies charged with local economic development in developing regions such as small island states. Policy makers in these regions need to close the gaps in the research and data around the impact and importance of digital-creative sectors in sustainable development, as well as highlight those important creative spillovers that can support innovation across more traditionally dominant sectors such as the Blue Economy.

So, although the creative industries are now widely recognised for their ability to positively differentiate and impact on the competitive advantage of cities, regions and countries, the implementation in local and national policy making to support this impact is still variable (Bakshi et al., 2013).

Recognition by national government, non-governmental organisations and research bodies of the importance of creative cluster development in these regions is often lacking, with the perceived importance of urban agglomeration then becoming a major limiting factor in the support made available by local policy makers to creative cluster initiatives.

A case study of the Platform Moving Image Cluster

This case study of the Platform cluster responds to the concepts discussed earlier by exploring how a cluster in a smaller city, based in a largely rural region that lacks the breadth and structures of established screen industry clusters, is developed, evolves and becomes embedded in place. The geographical nature of this small city location also provides some interesting parallels with many dispersed or archipelagic SIDS.

Platform is the moving image cluster for Stoke on Trent and Staffordshire in the UK and is based at Staffordshire University in the city of Stoke on Trent. The cluster works without a central physical 'hub' and, indeed, without even a traditional city centre in which to locate.

The city lacks a traditional metropolitan centre, with the city of Stoke on Trent actually being comprised of six towns, spatially linear and each with its own identifiable town centre, town hall, history and identity. Defining a hub then was not only problematic but perhaps unhelpful in terms of engaging companies and creative practitioners across the whole city.

Stoke on Trent has suffered a decline in population over the last 30 years with that trend only recently beginning to slowly reverse. The city has seen a well-documented decline in its population, its level of skilled employment and its educational attainment (Mahoney & Kearon, 2018). It has one of the highest proportion of unskilled and manual labour as a percentage of its workforce in the UK (Office for National Statistics, 2019) and a fragile start-up ecosystem.

There was some start-up support provided by Staffordshire University for students and a small amount of low-cost incubator space, but the vital sector-specific business support, accelerator schemes and access to scale up finance were still lacking.

Key to the growth of the screen sector in the region has been the presence of high-quality and high-reputation undergraduate degree courses at Staffordshire University, based centrally in the city of Stoke on Trent. The role that universities play in building sustainable creative economies has been recognised for some time (Garlick, 1998: Atkinson & Easthope, 2008), but increasingly, it is not just sector-specific research and graduate talent that drives this sector growth. For a region like Stoke on Trent and Staffordshire that has lacked the history of production and subsequent support infrastructure around the digital-creative industries, the presence of an anchor institution such as Staffordshire University has been central to this growth.

The strength of the graduates from these courses has provided the basis for the growth of the sector, not only attracting young people from around the country to the region but crucially encouraging some of these graduates to stay. This is then supported by a successful and long-standing university start-up programme that offers seed funding and general business mentoring in the initial phases of the graduate company. The infrastructure of the sector then has grown up around the output of graduates from these film and media courses.

As the film and media courses have produced high skill graduates over the last 15–20 years, there has been a slow but steady increase in the levels of start-ups, micro companies and freelancers working in the moving image sector in the city region. Staffordshire does not have a history of extensive production in the moving image industries. However, in the last ten years, more feature films and TV programmes have shot in the region, and this has led to more visibility and an increase in capacity. This increase in capacity has seen feature productions moving into the county along with increased graduate retention due to the building of a critical mass of companies, skilled crew and a more outward-looking local authority.

In 2008 the feature film *Soulboy* shot in and around Stoke on Trent, kick-starting the process of building the city and the region as a location for production. Following the success of the film, the Stoke Film Office was created and the local animation and film festival was successfully rebranded as the Stoke Your Fires Film Festival, attracting local and international filmmakers to the city.

The region is blessed with outstanding locations ranging from the natural beauty of the Staffordshire Moorlands to the urban streets of Stoke on Trent. Its easily accessible position in terms of both excellent road and rail networks gives it easy proximity to Manchester and Birmingham. The main rail terminal at Stoke on Trent also means that central London is reachable in 90 minutes. However, the region also lacks significantly in high-end production facilities and infrastructure, meaning that equipment hire, studio space and post-production facilities are all accessed outside the region.

There is also a lack of positions being made available to crew and SMEs in the region when these productions shoot there. Whether this is due to a perceived lack of experienced crew on behalf of the productions or an actual lack needs further investigating.

The growth of production SMEs and individual writer/director/producers in the region over the last ten years, mainly founded by university graduates, started to attract other businesses into the region. Location services, costume design and supply and business support services for the sector were all gradually locating in the Staffordshire region. The importance of a university centrally located in the city with a strong reputation in the digital-creative sector therefore cannot be overstated for the development of the cluster as a whole (Mateos-Garcia & Sapsed, 2012).

Moving image sector SMEs in the county now number more than 160, consisting of corporate, feature, documentary and animation production companies, along with a number of related suppliers such as location services, talent agencies and costume designers. The figures on the number of freelance and sole trader workers are less clear and need further research to establish the true scale of the cluster.

The scale of this cluster then compares very favourably with concepts of workable critical mass (Chapain & De Propis, 2009) and was built around the recognised ideal scenario, outlined in the EU Cluster Excellence Framework, for cluster development with the region, having strong sector-specific university and/or research institute ties, a critical mass of core sector companies and a hinterland of related subcontractors and service providers (Federal Ministry of Economics and Technology, Germany, 2009).

The development of the cluster has not though been a simple process, and there has been tension between building and marketing the city as a city of film and television production, and its heritage as a centre of ceramics. There are dangers in seeing places as simply associated with specific creative sectors, Stoke on Trent and its history of ceramic craftsmanship being particularly relevant. Indeed, over-reliance on place-based heritage production often stifles the uptake of new industries, those based on digital technologies such as the Platform cluster, in local growth plans. This is particularly relevant to developing regions as 'creative industries' are often associated with heritage crafts, and it is important that in capacity-building in these regions, clearer understandings of the breadth of the creative industries are built with policy makers, researchers and practitioners.

A catalytic moment in the understanding of creative and cultural sectors, particularly those based around digital technologies, was the multi-partner collaboration formed to bid for the UK City of Culture 2021. Platform provided substantial insights and linkages into the moving image sector that saw the city shortlisted and then into the final group of cities that were asked to present to the City of Culture panel. Although not successful in being awarded the title, the engagement of Platform and the moving image sector saw an important shift in the understanding of these sectors to the economic and social life of the city.

The conditions then for a cluster-like Platform to fully develop and thrive comes not just from the co-location of SMEs but from the surrounding conditions that lead to that agglomeration (Ache, 2000). This is a slightly differentiated approach to cluster development from that of more classical writings, where a specific regional or geographical condition was not seen as important, to a recognition of 'place-based' factors being important to cluster development. This model suggests that the local environment can be as much of an entrepreneur and innovator as the individual firm. This then obviously has substantial importance for local policy makers in so much as the recognition of place-based factors, and the necessary support to build these, becomes vital in creative cluster development (European Commission, 2016).

In regions like Stoke on Trent and Staffordshire, where the lack of a major city could be seen as a limiting factor, this approach takes even greater importance. Creative clusters then can be seen as the product not only of geographical co-location but also of the place-based social, economic and cultural conditions of its production. There is a bi-directional and co-constitutional dynamic here then where clusters are created by specific place-based factors but then in turn, impact on and change the nature of that place through their impact on its economic, social and cultural fabric.

It could be argued that for Stoke on Trent, creative heritage, in this case with the ceramics industry, can be seen as part of a fabric of creative innovation, a place-based DNA that impacts the development of enterprises in the region. However, this description fails to recognise the distinction between a traditional and an emerging sector. Whilst ceramics industries in the region quite naturally use that heritage as part of their development, for the emerging digital-creative sector in the city region, the opposite is true. The ceramics sector often brands itself on the traditional craft skills of its manufacturing process, similar to the way in which the concept of *manufacture* is used as an indication of quality, creativity and craftsmanship in the long-established companies of the Swiss watchmaking industry.

The moving image sector however highlights its strengths through the use and development of the latest digital technology. Rather than craft skills, SMEs, universities and larger companies brand their competitive advantage through being at the cutting edge of production techniques – technology, not heritage, being the differentiator. What has developed more recently for the ceramics sector is the growth of advanced materials science and technology that uses ceramics production for a multitude of high-technology applications. The crossover here then mirrors the impact of digital technologies on the creative and cultural sectors.

So, whilst Platform can be seen as a creative cluster based in a city region that has a heritage of innovation and creative manufacturing – and therefore benefiting from that association – the actual value of that relationship to place and heritage is debatable. The dynamics then of place-based impacts on cluster developments are more complex than perhaps first perceived. Place can help and hinder cluster development at the same time, depending on the nature of the locality. That cliché of 'place matters' actually does ring true although not perhaps in the way that it is normally used.

There is then, it seems, something of a dialectical nature to the opposing yet co-constitutional forces in play when clusters become established in a specific region, draw on its industrial heritage, but seek to re-imagine it in a different direction.

The nature of creative hubs

In finding a cluster model that would work for Stoke on Trent and its wider region then, the particular nature of its place had to be factored in. As discussed previously, the notion of 'place' is highly complex and not reducible to the marketing terminology of city branders. It is important in understanding how a cluster will work in practice and how it will engage the sector. The engagement often takes the form of a recognised 'creative quarter' in a city, or a centralised and physical hub for specific cluster meetings, activities and the more generalised ad hoc sector community.

Clusters in cities can often be located in small areas, such as the shirt makers of Jermyn Street and the suit makers of Saville Row in London, the single block 'diamond district' of West 47th Street in New York or the San Salvario district in Turin. Such co-location is typical of creative clusters in particular, but in establishing Platform, the spatial characteristics of Stoke on Trent, with a population of around 260,000 spread out over nearly a hundred square kilometres, meant a rethinking of traditional cluster and hub approaches.

The nature and history of the individual towns of Stoke on Trent would problematise any decision around where to locate a creative hub. In the early development stages of Platform, a decision was made not to develop a central hub for the cluster, based on the nature of the city and city region and its particular geographical and cultural construction. This decision goes against many of the accepted wisdoms around the importance of hubs as a driver of local creative economies (Virani et al., 2016; Ahton & Comunian, 2019).

The rise of the 'creative hub' over the last 20 years and this accepted wisdom have come about despite the difficulties of quantifying their specific value or return on investment. Like clusters, the concept and terminology of hubs have become quite ubiquitous. Physical hubs are predominantly located in urban centres, often have a virtual element to them and become recognised centres for freelance workers, micro and small companies, non-profits and academics to come together and collaborate. Done well, with multi-agency stakeholder involvement and commitment, these hubs can be transformative.

However, their perception and implementation can also be limiting and conflated with many other concepts such as creative quarters and creative cities. There has also been a historical focus on hubs being primarily physical buildings, and whilst the ability to bring people together face to face has been central to creative collaboration and innovation, the value of creative hubs extends beyond simply a café and meeting places.

Hubs have traditionally been a vital part of any creative cluster initiative, the relationship between the wider regional cluster – which may extend over a significant geographical area – and the hub or central meeting place being of real importance. Cluster initiatives in particular have stressed the importance of developing a recognised place for meeting, sharing stories and projects, creating collaborations and being a vibrant venue in which to engage the wider business and social community. Implementing this in a large urban centre is relatively easy and may explain why so much funding and investment go into the numerous city hubs – outputs are easier to achieve and to measure.

For those 'other' geographies, particularly small island states and archipelagos however, that cluster and hub model can be not just difficult but impossible to implement.

The research and work conducted in the Eastern Caribbean showed dispersed creative populations, activity and innovation popping up in different locations at different times. Picking one island in this region then as the location for the cluster hub would not only prove economically and politically difficult but also, by its very nature, draw talent and investment away from the other islands where micro but dynamic networks may already be forming.

The nature of travel in these regions also means that it is far more difficult to move easily between islands and therefore be part of a creative community if it is purely centred on a single island hub. The effect of this is actually to marginalise the creative workforce and community across the majority of the region – the 'hub' only really being of value to those on that particular island. The key driver for hubs in urban spaces, that they are an easily accessible, centrally located place for creatives to congregate on a regular basis and therefore share those knowledge and experience spillovers, becomes the very thing that makes it a negative for small island states.

This may go some way in explaining why previous attempts at creating cluster initiatives in regions such as the Caribbean and Pacific islands have struggled to be sustainable and to engage the population they were designed to serve. Much of the work around Caribbean clusters in particular has stressed the importance and benefits of clusters to the region, mapped any sector concentrations and recommended action yet has failed to examine the process of engagement in the cluster by the sector itself. The effectiveness of any cluster initiative is dependent on its design and implementation in relation to the specifics of the location, sector and social/economic/cultural conditions.

Clusters in SIDS

To find a way forward, it is worth going back to the Platform case study. Interestingly, there are parallels between the development of a creative cluster in a polycentric and peri-urban region like Stoke on Trent, and many developing countries, particularly those with dispersed populations and small urban centres, such as in SIDS. The Eastern Caribbean, for example, comprises of an arc of small islands stretching from Puerto Rico in the north down to Granada, each being a sovereign country with its own identifiable culture and economy. Although larger and more populous than the city of Stoke on Trent, the nature of its physical and cultural geography is similar. This also mirrors the archipelagic structure of the Maldives Islands, with a current population of around 540,000 spread over 185 inhabited islands (UNDESA, 2020).

This research was presented to the United Nations Conference on Trade and Development (UNCTAD) Expert Group meeting in Geneva in October 2019 as part of its ongoing Creative Economy development strategy. This work then, although regionally and locally focused, has important implications for creative cluster development internationally, particularly in regions that seem untenable for creating workable and sustainable clusters.

Since 2014 I have worked with young filmmakers and creative entrepreneurs in the Eastern Caribbean, as well as supporting the OECS in its work to develop the digital-creative sector across the region. The Caribbean has a number of local, regional clusters, along with two inter-Caribbean clusters – in animation and maritime services. Organic clustering can be seen at work in SIDS in Trinidad and Tobago with the various industries of the well-established and globally recognised Carnival (Burke, 2014).

In 2017, Compete Caribbean and the Inter-American Development Bank issued a call for expressions of interest around the development of a cluster strategy for the region; yet a strong cluster initiative in response to this action has so far failed to emerge.

The OECS is also attempting to bring a unified voice to this region through a programme of economic harmonisation, in partnership with the Caribbean Development Bank and the Inter-American Development Bank amongst others. In 2017 the Caribbean Development Bank launched the Creative and Cultural Industries Innovation Fund, with an initial capitalisation of US$2.6 million and the aim of supporting the growth of a creative industries sector across the Caribbean. Significant sums have had to be allocated to the Covid-19 response however, and it is unclear at this stage how the innovation fund will impact the sector in the region.

This support for creative industries in SIDS regions is unfortunately not typical however. Programmes of creative industries and creative cluster development have been attempted in the Pacific Islands over the last five or six years, yet none have succeeded in gaining enough traction to make a significant impact or to be sustainable. This may be explainable in part due to the focus on creative industries as cultural heritage, as opposed to the opportunities of new digital-creative entrepreneurship.

The Indian Ocean as well lags some way behind the Caribbean in developing creative economy projects, clusters and initiatives but offers a potentially interesting and viable test bed for a polycentric creative cluster that engages a dispersed population. The Maldives, for example, chain of 1192 islands grouped into 26 atolls, is spread over 90,000 square kilometres and has geospatial properties that are similar to the Eastern Caribbean.

In looking at how a creative cluster might be developed, in both the Eastern Caribbean and the Maldives archipelago, the experience of the Platform cluster and the concept of a dispersed cluster could offer a way forward.

New model clusters: dispersion and moveable hubs

It is clear from the design, development and success of the Platform cluster that, if cluster initiatives are to work in small island states such as those mentioned earlier, are to be sustainable and then have significant impact, the old model of city-based creative clusters, centred around a single physical hub, has to be reworked. What is required is a cluster model where the cluster itself continually makes and remakes itself in line with the activity and needs of the sector across the region. To engage the sector across all the islands or atolls and to deliver support and energy where and when it is required, those traditional models of cluster dynamics and centralised hubs are not appropriate.

We could therefore envisage, as with the Platform cluster, a hub that has no fixed location, becoming moveable and mobile, avoiding the constraints and difficulties of being based in a single island. One model that could be appropriated comes from wireless communication networks.

Mobile Adhoc Networks, or MANETs, are a decentralised type of wireless network where independent devices can create and join a mobile network 'on the fly' and without the infrastructural restrictions of fixed routers and wired networks. The decentralised nature of wireless ad hoc networks makes them suitable for a variety of applications where central nodes can't be relied on and may improve the scalability of networks compared to wireless-managed networks. Minimal configuration and quick deployment make ad hoc networks suitable for emergency situations like natural disasters or military conflicts. The dynamic and adaptive nature of these networks of nodes allows them to form and reform quickly, responding to needs as they occur.

These nodes can freely create and dynamically self-organise a temporary wireless network among themselves, allowing people and devices to seamlessly internetwork in areas with no pre-existing communication infrastructure or administrative support, unlike conventional wireless fixed networks.

This model of dynamic networking offers the possibility of being applied to how individuals, micro and small companies can connect, collaborate and innovate across geographically dispersed, polycentric regions. The concept of a mobile and moveable 'hub' then becomes a function of the dynamic networks that are in place in SIDS regions. The 'moveable hub' provides an impetus for the creation of a temporary node on an individual island before moving to the next island, either in response to activity or as part of a strategic network outreach programme.

The benefit of this is the low-cost, flexible nature of operation, without the need for investment in fixed, physical buildings, the inclusive and non-partisan nature of the hub, particularly important for working across national or regional borders, and the ability to quickly respond to changes in national or regional policy, economic activity or uncertainty and unexpected challenges such as the Covid-19 pandemic.

This model of using the theory of MANETs to understand how polycentric clusters and mobile hubs can link small island states also has possible connections to concepts of a global cluster network (Turkina & Van Assche, 2017). This theory sees clusters as nodes in a global network of clusters, connected to each other through horizontal partnerships – linkages between firms in similar value chain activities – and vertical buyer–supplier connections between companies in different value chain stages.

However, this could be seen to conflate basic commercial and trade networks with cluster initiatives. The Hollywood entertainment cluster in Los Angeles, for example, has many close links, partnerships and commercial collaborations with the West London film cluster in the UK. This however is not a cluster collaboration in and of itself but a connective business network of companies that come together to develop, produce and distribute specific projects and products.

Companies can have international supply chain networks and connect with companies in a number of regions or countries without this necessarily being classed as a cluster. It is the functioning of the cluster initiative as an enabler of collaborative innovation and knowledge exchange between companies, along with the regional and 'place' advocacy, that marks clusters from simply commercial networks.

The concept behind the nodes of a global cluster, or a cluster of clusters, however has some relevance to the multi-state agencies of SIDS regions such as the OECS, the Global Island Partnership (GLISPA), the Indian Ocean Rim Association (IORA) and the Pacific Islands Forum (PIF). The geographical, social and economic similarities between island nations in these regions could allow for a more workable multi-region and multi-state cluster to be formed. For example, a global network of clusters based in small island states and focused on the digital screen industries can have benefits for producers in these regions. It could allow for a collaborative approach to production and distribution with creative entrepreneurs who understand the challenges that these particular locations need to address.

This concept links to the earlier discussion of how hubs can be seen as nodes in a temporary and flexible network that responds to the demands of dispersed activity. Scaling this up to a wider regional or global network then has possibilities. The key here though is the application of this concept in the real world. Theoretical approaches to clusters and innovation networks often fail in real-world application due to the lack of commercial experience and understanding of the theorist, the inability to then take the concept through to testing and implementation and, consequently, to have any real impact.

The value of the research into the Platform cluster in Stoke on Trent is that the concept of a decentralised cluster and a moveable hub has been put into practice, tested and evaluated. Whilst there are certainly challenges in implementing a model like this, Platform has provided evidence of real-world impact of such a model and the concrete benefits to micro and small screen–based companies in the region. Transferring such a model to creative clusters and hubs in SIDS then has a precedent and an exemplar to build on.

Conclusion

Whilst the traditional concept of clusters and hubs seems to be far from applicable to the human and physical geography of many SIDS, the reworking of these traditional models into the ideas of dispersed clusters and moveable hubs presents an innovative but implementable way forward.

The crux of this of course is in the application of a theoretical model to real-world needs and challenges, and that is where the case study of Platform proves valuable. The concept of dynamic nodes with a cluster network has been shown to work with that cluster, and whilst there are obvious obstacles to scaling this up to SIDS regions, it has the possibility of allowing transformative networks of collaborative learning and innovation to develop in regions where these possibilities are often dismissed.

By investing in developing and implementing these models, both financially and politically, the benefits that clusters and creative hubs can bring to digital, knowledge-based, creative sectors in SIDS are obvious. It enables entrepreneurs in regions not normally seen as being workable for such networks to come together, collaborate and build stronger and more vibrant creative economies.

References

Ache, P. 2000. Vision and Creativity: Challenge for City Regions. *Futures*, 32(5), June, pp. 435–449.

Ahton, D. & Comunian, R. 2019. Universities as Creative Hubs: Modes and Practices in the UK Context. In *Creative Hubs in Question*, pp. 359–379. Palgrave Macmillan, London.

Atkinson, R. & Easthope, H. 2008. The Creative Class in Utero? The Australian City, the Creative Economy and the Role of Higher Education. *Built Environment*, 34(3), pp. 307–318.

Bakshi, H., Hargreaves, I. & Mateos-Garcia, J. 2013. *A Manifesto for the Creative Economy*. NESTA, London.

Bakshi, H. & Mateos-Garcia, J. 2016. *The Geography of Creativity in the UK*. NESTA, London.

Burke, S. 2014. Creative Clustering in Small Island States: The Case of Trinidad and Tobago's Carnival Industry. *Caribbean Quarterly*, 60(1), pp. 74–95.

Chapain, C. & Comunian, R. 2010. Enabling and Inhibiting the Creative Economy: The Role of the Local and Regional Dimensions in England. *Regional Studies*, 44(6), pp. 717–734.

Chapain, C., Cooke, P., De Propris, L., MacNeill, S. & Mateos-Garcia, J. 2010. *Creative Clusters and Innovation: Putting Creativity on the Map*. NESTA, London.

Chapain, C. & De Propis, L. 2009. Drivers and Processes of Creative Industries in Cities and Regions. *Creative Industries Journal*, 2(1), pp. 9–18.

Cole, A. 2008. Distant Neighbors: The New Geography of Animated Film Production in Europe. *Regional Studies*, 42, pp. 1–14.

Comunian, R., Chapain, C. & Clifton, N. 2010. Location, Location, Location: Exploring the Complex Relationship between Creative Industries and Place. *Creative Industries Journal*, 3(1), pp. 5–10.

Dijkstra, L., Garcilaz, E. & McCann, P. 2013. The Economic Performance of European Cities and City Regions: Myths and Realities. *European Planning Studies*, 21(3), pp. 334–354.

European Commission. 2016. *Smart Guide to Cluster Policy*. Directorate-General for Internal Market, Industry, Entrepreneurship and SMEs, Brussels. Accessed at http://ec.europa.eu/growth/smes/cluster/

European Creative and Cultural Industries Alliance. 2012. *Developing Successful Creative & Cultural Clusters*. ECCIA, Brussels.

European Creative and Cultural Industries Alliance. 2014. *Best Practices for Building Creative Cluster Coworking Centres*. ECCIA, Brussels.

Federal Ministry of Economics and Technology. 2009. *Cluster Management Excellence Volume 1*. Network Services, Germany.

Ferilli, G., Sacco, P.L. & Tavano Blessi, G. 2012. *Cities as Creative Hubs: From Instrumental to Functional Values of Culture-Led Local Development*, pp. 245–270. Ashgate and Sustainable City and Creativity, Farnham.

Foord, J. 2009. Strategies for Creative Industries: An International Review. *Creative Industries Journal*, 1(2), pp. 91–113.

Fundeanu, D. & Badele, C. 2014. The Impact of Regional Innovative Clusters on Competitiveness. *Procedia, Social and Behavioural Sciences*, March, pp. 405–414.

Garlick, S.C. 1998. Creative Associations in Special Places: Enhancing the Partnership Role of Universities in Building Competitive Regional Economies. *Evaluations and Investigations Programme, Higher Education Division,* 1(3), pp. 203–210.

Hermans, J., Castiaux, A., Dejardin, M. & Lucas, S. 2010. Configuration in the Flesh: Challenges in Publicly Promoted Clusters. *The Journal of Technology Transfer*, 37(5), pp. 609–630.

Ketels, C., Lindqvist, G. & Solvell, O. 2006. *Cluster Initiatives in Developing and Transition Economies*. Center for Strategy and Competitiveness, Stockholm, 1st edition, May.

Kong, L. 2012. Improbable Art: The Creative Economy and Sustainable Cluster Development in a Hong Kong Industrial District. *Eurasian Geography and Economics*, 53(2), pp. 182–196.

Lazzaretti, L., Boix, R. & Capone, F. 2009. Why Do Creative Industries Cluster? IERMB Working Paper in Economics, no. 09.02, April 2009.

Leunig, T. & Overman, H. 2008 Spatial Patterns of Development and the British Housing Market. *Oxford Review of Economic Policy*, 24(1), pp. 59–78.

Mahoney, I. & Kearon, T. 2018. Social Quality and Brexit in Stoke on Trent, England. *The International Journal of Social Quality*, 8(1), pp. 1–20.

Mateos-Garcia, J., Klinger, J. & Stathoulopoulos, K. 2018. *Creative Nation, How the Creative Industries Are Powering the UK's Nations and Regions*. NESTA. London.

Mateos-Garcia, J. & Sapsed, J. 2012. *The Role of Universities in Enhancing Creative Clustering*. CENTRIM, University of Brighton.

Office for National Statistics. 2019. *Regional Labour Market Statistics in the UK: September 2019*. Office for National Statistics, London.

Oksanen, K. & Stahle, P. 2013. Physical Environment as a Source for Innovation: Investigating the Attributes of Innovative Space. *Journal of Knowledge Management*, 17(6), pp. 815–827.

Porter, M. & Stern, S. 2001. Location Matters. *MIT Sloan Management Review*, 42(4), Summer.

Turkina, E. & Van Assche, A. 2017. Global Connectedness and Local Innovation in Industrial Clusters. *Journal of International Business Studies*, 49(6), pp. 706–728.

United Nations Department of Economic and Social Affairs. 2020. *World Population Prospects, 2019 Revision*. UNDESA, Geneva. Accessed at www.population.un.org/wpp/publications.

Virani, T., Dovey, J., Pratt, A., Lansdowne, J., Moreton, S. & Merkel, J. 2016. *Creative Hubs: Understanding the New Economy*. British Council, London.

5   Island states, innovation and redefining the helix

Introduction

The need for innovation in solving the considerable sustainable development issues faced by SIDS is perhaps more acute and urgent than ever. The Covid-19 pandemic has highlighted the fragility of island economies centred almost exclusively on the Blue Economy, and many island governments are now struggling with significantly reduced foreign revenues coupled with rising national debt. Making their economies more resilient by driving island-based innovation then is not just desirable but now absolutely critical.

Fundamentally, innovation is the transformation of new ideas into economic and social solutions (Navarro et al., 2016; Crespi et al., 2014).

It can be seen in new, more efficient means of production, new channels or methods of distribution, the new business models associated with such innovations or the organisational or relational aspects of business and social structures (Gault, 2010).

Whilst innovation has traditionally been linked with technical, scientific and technology-based solutions, other areas such as creative, aesthetic or service-based improvements have also been discussed, what Stoneman (2010) defines as soft innovation.

Miles and Green (2008) highlight that this can most clearly be seen in the creative and cultural sectors where the final output is aesthetic and not functional, such as those outputs from the music, fashion or film and television sectors, and those creative industries companies are often more innovative than the rest of the economy, including firms in knowledge-intensive sectors (Muller et al., 2009).

The lines between these areas of innovation however are blurring to the point of disappearing. The fashion industry, for example, has for some time innovated around the development, design and incorporation of technical fabrics into their clothing ranges and have done so in partnership with more traditional science and technology firms.

The process of automotive design and manufacture is often seen as involving technical innovation, with the creative aspect of the process merely seen in the aesthetics of any new model. However, the design process is increasingly impacted by immersive and pre-visualisation technologies, derived from implementing the creative technologies and processes of visual effects techniques from motion picture production.

The crossovers between the digital-creative economy, technology and scientific innovation are increasingly complex and interdependent, so the definition of soft innovation as something apart from other forms of innovation is losing its importance. The creative industries have impacted across the innovation landscape in terms of process and application but also drive the need for technology innovation through the consumer demand for better and more powerful information and communication technologies.

Also, as soft innovation describes a process of aesthetic creation as well as creative process innovation, it is open to the arguments around the conflation of creative actions and innovation. Creative activity is not necessarily innovation, so applying the terminology of soft innovation to the creative and cultural sectors often tends to obscure some more profound ideas of creative innovation. This is because, as we've seen in the examples earlier, it is often the link and intersections between technology, creativity, product and process that the creative industries can drive the most.

In the 1960s, NASA commissioned lens maker Carl Zeiss to design and manufacture a fast camera lens that could be used to capture the far side of the moon during the Apollo mission in 1966. That Carl Zeiss Planar 50 mm f0.7 was then used by film director Stanley Kubrick to achieve a certain visual style in the 1975 film Barry Lyndon. He had to design a new camera body and focus mechanism to allow the lens to work properly for a cinematographer.

That technical and creative-aesthetic innovation then went on to be highly influential in the design of consumer and professional optics across many fields, driven by other filmmakers and photographers who saw Kubrick's results and wanted to emulate that visual style.

So applying the terminology of soft innovation to the creative sectors to understand their innovation processes and dynamics can be misleading. Rather, it is understanding that a strong creative ecosystem is not simply about creative innovation with the sector but that it provides an innovation environment in which cross-sector work can be initiated.

The Triple Helix

That innovation environment, as a mechanism for driving and supporting innovation has been framed most notably in the concept of the Triple Helix (Etzkowitz & Leyesdorff, 1995). This model of innovation describes how industry, government and universities can interact to foster economic and social innovation and development (Figure 5.1).

Dzisah and Etzkowitz (2008) argue that the Triple Helix is based on the premise that the university plays a leading role in this model. Their premise is that higher education institutions are virtually everywhere and their flexible nature allows them to fill a variety of roles, well beyond their traditional activities. Whilst theoretically this might be true, in practice, and certainly when it is applied to the

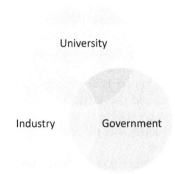

University

Industry   Government

Figure 5.1 The Triple Helix

creative and cultural industries, the reality of its implementation and impact on the ground is often far from this theorised ideal.

The 'flexible nature' of universities is also perhaps something of a misnomer, with 'varying' being a better word. Universities certainly do engage in a variety of functions – essentially research and teaching and learning, but to call them flexible seems to be based more in wish-fulfilment than in reality.

Extensive bureaucratic, policy-driven processes and complex, highly competitive, academic departments make for an organisation that is anything but responsive and flexible. Whilst many industries have seen transformative disruption through technology and business model innovation, higher education has proved to be resistant to such disruption in any meaningful way.

If these inherent structures and practices then make it difficult to manifest any real innovation within universities, it is not surprising that their engagement with industry and their theorised role in the Triple Helix have remained resistant to significant change. This presents a real problem for the creative and cultural sectors, as Crossick (2006) and Cruz et al. (2019) have noted, and is linked to the largely urban-based, developed world positioning of the Triple Helix and the hierarchical positioning of the university within it.

We saw in the chapter on clusters beyond the city the limiting association of creative, digital and knowledge-based economies with large urban centres, and this is mirrored in the approach to regional innovation strategies and the application of helix models. The assumption is that Triple Helix innovation policies and strategies, designed largely by and for research-intensive and well-resourced urban universities, work best in, and therefore need to be focused on, the city. The concept of the Triple Helix is an example of how urban-centric theory follows through into strategy and policy without examining the exclusionary nature of such a focus.

Understanding the nature of the Triple Helix then, as it applies to the creative industries and their rapid integration into many other industrial fields, is going to mean a reworking of Etzkowitz and Leydesdorff's original model (1995). In particular, we need to re-examine and reformulate the role of universities, to go beyond the ideas of knowledge transfer (KT) as the framework for how universities engage with industry and to decouple innovation from the language of science and technology.

This final point is crucial to implementing this whole process, not just from a university point of view but for how the whole helix model is structured and implemented. Given the rapid rise of the creative and cultural industries as a major global economic force, one might expect to see a resulting rise in the academic and political engagement with the creative sector and its role in the innovation ecosystem.

However, as Heidemann Lassen et al. (2018) have noted, for the majority of creative and cultural entrepreneurs, SMEs and actors, contact with universities has remained sparse, with few active collaborations. Cruz et al. (2019) pose the question as to what motivates this lack of engagement, given the political importance and visibility of both knowledge transfer and the creative sectors in the policies of many developed countries and regions.

The answer is not a simple one but comes back to the theorising and resultant policy and strategy interventions around innovation. This is more than just semantics. It is the fundamental language used to describe innovation, what it is and where its importance lies.

The linguistic coupling of science and technology to innovation, along with the principles and strategies of knowledge transfer, immediately alienates the creative and cultural sectors and distances them from research institutions.

This is then reinforced by the priorities of government and research funding bodies with the consequence that researchers continue to develop research projects, partnerships and outcomes along familiar lines in order to attract funding.

There are numerous examples of this not only in academic literature but also, and perhaps more importantly, in government departments and non-governmental, international organisations. This is particularly true of strategies around SIDS. One can see this, for example, in blogs on the United Nations Sustainable Development Goals website. Whilst one can see a recognition that it is entrepreneurship and innovation in new sectors that will boost productive activities in these regions, it is rarely followed through with discussions beyond innovating in tourism, blue economies or clean energy. It is vital to recognise how this approach can restrict the thinking around innovation and negatively impact the development of new, sustainable sectors for island growth and security.

Universities still have an important role to play here though. Their engagement with the creative and cultural sectors is often confined to what is called the 'third mission', a description of a social and community-based role that sees the university as an active player in its city or region on more than just a research and teaching and learning platform. Whilst this third mission is actively engaged with KT, it again tends to focus on the technical knowledge-intensive fields (Crossick, 2006).

The rebranding of this third mission to a wider description of the 'civic university' has gone some way to rebalancing the understanding of research, innovation and the creative sectors, but that is yet to be made concrete. The concept though of the 'civic university' may be more than just the branding exercise that it appears to be, and nowhere might this be more important that in developing regions such as small island states.

The Triple Helix and creative industries: education, knowledge and innovation beyond universities

The Triple Helix positions the university as having a leading role in regional economic development, particularly in cities, and suggests that this primacy is further enhanced in knowledge-based economies, as these institutions have the research and knowledge capability to drive innovation (Fernandez-Esquinas & Pinto, 2014; Drucker & Goldstein, 2007). This transfer of knowledge from a university to industry in a Triple Helix is seen as being particularly important in clusters and innovation ecosystems in urban centres (Viale & Campodall' Orto, 2002).

The problem with this argument is, as we've seen, that it is insufficiently granular to take into account variances across and between industrial sectors and, in particular, the digital-creative and cultural industries. Whilst the 'creative city' is portrayed as the natural home for creative and cultural sector growth and innovation, the characteristics and business models of the creative industries do not lend themselves to the typically science- and technology-focused theorising of the Triple Helix.

This then needs rethinking. The role of the university in creative clusters and regions and Triple Helix relations becomes less knowledge transfer in the traditional sense and more about networking, enabling and connecting peers.

Approaching the helix in this way allows the creative and cultural sectors to fully exploit the significant tacit knowledge, symbolic knowledge and the sizeable intrinsic value that the sector is based upon, rather than having to fit traditional helixical structures and roles. The creative sectors have very different spatial-economic models for innovation, collaboration and knowledge sharing that are often fluid, casual and multi-dimensional. These then can often pose problems for the more formal collaborative structures of universities and other industries (Jeannerat & Crevoiser, 2016). This is exemplified in the numerous examples of Triple Helixes found in advanced science and technology disciplines rather than in the creative and cultural sectors (Viale & Campodall'Orto, 2002).

However, it is important here not to conflate creation with innovation as creative sectors have long had informal working relationships with universities. It is the nature of the relationship that differs from the widely theorised Triple Helix model, being informal and often outside university-designed and university-managed project structures. Creative practitioners often work as part-time academics, and full-time academics often have their own creative and cultural practices that feed naturally into their teaching and learning, as well as their published research. This is not the same as innovation relationships, so defining this as part of a creative Triple Helix can be problematic. This is especially marked in smaller cities and ecosystems where many creative workers operate in multiple roles (Granger & Hamilton, 2010).

Other arguments for the positioning of universities as a primary actor in the helix is that they can be particularly useful in accelerating the process of learning, networking and interdependency in advanced clusters and ecosystems (Viale & Campodall'Orto, 2002).

This argument is still however based on a framework of 'knowledge transfer' and the hierarchical positioning of a university in that helix, which, for the characteristics and working practices of the creative and cultural industries, is not compatible. So whilst the Triple Helix model has been, and still is, used extensively as a policy and strategy tool for city and regional development, its effectiveness is notably diminished if we try to apply this to cities or regions with significant creative clusters.

Granger (2018) in her case study of creative industries and their relation to local universities in the UK city of Leicester found some interesting but not wholly surprising results. When asked the question 'Where does your organisation secure new knowledge for innovation?', it is interesting to note that 93 practitioners (89.4%) indicated that these were found principally within the industry, whilst 87 respondents (83.6%) cited the secondary importance of customers to innovation development.

So knowledge transfer or knowledge exchange in the creative industries – particularly those dominated by digital production and distribution such as film, television, games design, animation, visual effects – is often reversed, moving from industry to universities.

Innovation in these sectors is often driven by key players in the industry. As a result, the distinction between the main players (university–industry–customer–producer) and what is and isn't knowledge in context becomes more unclear.

In the creative industries, where micro-businesses are commonplace and where new skills can lose their competitiveness in a matter of months and become obsolete in a matter of years, the need for current skills, rapid response times and flexible collaboration is critical. These attributes are, however, not something that is typically seen in the vast majority of Triple Helix partnerships. For the creative and cultural industries, universities can play a significant role, but it has to be in a helix that is redefined and remodelled, not just for the creative industries but for the entirely different social, industrial and educational landscape in which we work.

The Triple Helix concept and its limitations in SIDS

The nature of small island states often makes traditional higher education institutions problematic in terms of population size, population dispersion or ease of travel for local people. Many states have no university provision, or have a small satellite campus from a larger, regional university. This is not to say, however, that this higher educational model cannot work for such regions.

The University of the West Indies provides a successful model of a dispersed campus that blends virtual and face-to-face learning. The university has physical campuses in Jamaica, Trinidad and Tobago, Barbados and Antigua and Barbuda. It also has the Open Campus, using the blended learning model and covering a wider scope of islands across the region.

Whilst this model provides a possible exemplar for small island tertiary education provision, it also, along with many other such institutions, tends to have a narrower curricula focus than universities on developed countries and large cities, often simply due to a lack of resource availability, both fiscal and human. Often the emphasis is on vocational education and training with limited engagement with external industry or innovation partners. In interviews with academic leaders at Seychelles University and Maldives National University, this point was emphasised as an area for development, particularly in light of the renewed focus on economic diversification following the 2020 pandemic.

Many of these institutions have a strong focus on teaching delivery with an underdeveloped research activity profile. The traditional model of the Triple Helix then is difficult to apply to these island states, and if local universities are to play a greater role in local economic development agendas, the way the helix is structured and applied for these regions needs to be rethought.

The business community is also far more limited than in developed countries, and larger cities are often geographically scattered, particularly in archipelagic regions, and insufficiently developed in terms of innovation support and management. These factors obviously impact the ability of small island nations to deliver strong innovation performance, but it is important to counter a persistent perception that because of these restrictions and the inability to sufficiently apply a Triple Helix model, small island states do not have the capacity or capability for significant innovation and locally incepted economic transformation.

The idea that a local community may play a significant role in creating an expanded or remodelled helix is something that Kolehmainen et al. (2016) discuss in terms of using the basic elements of the Triple Helix and applying a community-based, open innovation model to these remote or rural regions to create a quadruple helix. This has been further expanded to create a Quintuple Helix that incorporates aspects of sustainability (Grundel & Dahlstrom, 2016). The argument is that as the innovation-generating process of the Triple Helix has become more interactive, reflecting the nature of societal interactions, other actors and innovation partners join an expanding helix (Cavallini et al., 2016).

However, these additions, such as those of the end-user or customer as an element of the quadruple helix, are mostly superfluous. For example, most innovative companies already engage continuously with their markets to understand the potential of any innovation for their customers. This says more about the process of theorising the helix model than an understanding of its real-world application.

Reconceptualising the helix

We've seen how the concept of the Triple Helix has been extended to the quadruple, quintuple and sextuple helix, no doubt with further extensions currently being theorised. At the core of all these proposed extensions though is still the industry–university–government triad. All the follow-on extensions of the helix struggle to make concrete the definitions of the application of these additional actors, as well as the actual practical and on-the-ground roles and benefits of these extensions.

The actions at the core of the helix are also becoming less defined, with the prioritised role of the university in the helix becoming blurred and less easily quantifiable than it once was. The concept of knowledge transfer gave way to knowledge exchange as a way of bringing the relationship with industry up to date, but much of the theoretical work still prioritises academia as the centre of research and knowledge creation. We are seeing now, in many instances, that research primacy is being challenged and overtaken by industry partners that can act more swiftly, more decisively and with an ability to attract greater financial resources to a project. This does not mean that the university loses its relevance in the helix, but it does mean that the role is changing, with greater flexibility in its mission and an ability to respond more rapidly being a key requirement for success in the twenty-first century. We can see a similar shift in both industry and government.

In industry the relentless push for profit is now being challenged by the needs of the planet, of the requirement, increasingly driven by the consumer, to be aligned with the SDGs, and by the volatile global supply chains, financial markets and technology disruptions.

The shine of the 'fast-growing technology start-up' has diminished somewhat, with investors looking for greater alignment with impact as opposed simply to a fast exit and governments aware of the need for proper regulation and evidence of societal good before enacting fiscal incentives. Industry is having to pivot from a simple market-driven approach to one that is seen to be responsive and responsible. The ability of industry to align with the SDGs could, as we've seen, open up significant growth and profit potential, so it's not a case of one for the other but rather a recognition that a company's success needs to be built upon more than just driving shareholder value and vague, mission-aligned, CSR statements.

Likewise, governments at both national and sub-national levels are being challenged in unprecedented ways to deliver for their populations and communities.

Alongside this, the original helix and those subsequent variations have all failed to properly integrate the essential innovation element of national and international financial markets into the mix, a notable and surprising omission. The helix of the future then needs to be flexible in both its individual elements and their interactions. Above all, this new helix needs to be quick to respond, both upstream in its combination of inputs and actors and downstream in its applicability and impact.

The key question then is: 'How can the matrix of participants in the Triple Helix be reconfigured to better drive the economic and social development of developing regions and island economies, turning vulnerable and underperforming states and regions into sustainable, creative and knowledge-based economies?' The first step may be to examine the concept of agility and its role in product development and innovation in industry.

The principle of agility

The principles of the agile methodology originate in IT and software development, a process whereby progress is constantly assessed, problems highlighted and resolved quickly through lean experimentation and progress thereby does not get stalled.

This agility is based on self-organising teams, with a large degree of autonomy and not hindered by often slow-moving, top-down management. This approach improves quality and speed-to-market and is the antithesis of traditional command-and-control-style management. Whilst not applicable to many everyday business operations, it does find its most valuable use in the innovation process and in the bringing together of multi-skilled teams to address product, process or structural innovation (Brand et al., 2019).

These cross-functional teams do not necessarily require immediate and significant structural changes across an organisation but rather a change in the approach of teams themselves. Agile teams still require management, so, unlike the often sceptical assumptions of many C-suite executives that this approach leads to people 'just doing what they want', agile team supervision is about enabling the team to work together simultaneously as opposed to separately and sequentially (Rigby et al., 2016).

This model provides an innovative way in which the concept of the Triple Helix can be transformed into a dynamic structure more relevant and more actionable in the highly volatile commercial, societal and technological landscape of the twenty-first century.

The Agile Helix

Drawing on the previous discussion, the proposal then is to abandon the multiple extensions of the helix, which are cumbersome and problematic, not just theoretically but more importantly in real-world application, and to reconfigure the Triple Helix as the Agile Helix, a connected system of actors that is deliberately permeable to allow the ingress and egress of organisations, institutions, entrepreneurs, investors, end-users and communities. This sees the core of the helix as the three elements and does not extend the structure to 4, 5 or 6 elements as other models do. Instead, it sees the Triple Helix as a central organising framework around which both upstream and downstream actors and enablers can be integrated on a project-by-project or process-by-process basis (Figure 5.2).

Each element of the Agile Helix is able to apply its leverage flexibly and non-hierarchically in a dynamic system that connects to all the other helix actors in that particular project and location.

We've seen how important clusters can be in supporting collaborative innovation, and they can also play a vital role in an Agile Helix – that of the process facilitator. This role can also be taken on by any one of the three main actors, depending on the nature of the project. It can also bring in external expertise or assign facilitator roles to any outside organisation.

The purpose of the Agile Helix then is to make possible the undoubted benefits of the university–industry–government innovation trisect in situations where the normal role assignation is not practical or achievable. It especially frees up universities to be more flexible in the role that they can play. For universities without

Figure 5.2 The Agile Helix

extensive and well-resourced research capabilities, and therefore the output to drive the usual innovation flow sufficiently, the Agile Helix provides a framework for teaching and learning or civic-focused universities to still play an active part in the innovation process. For small island states, which often lack the level of higher education infrastructure and investment, the Agile Helix is a crucial innovation that brings all the benefits of connected and collaborative innovation to bear. In particular, it allows the flexibility of structures suited to the conditions and geographies of these regions and to integrate the all-important financial institutions and markets into the helix.

As discussed earlier, the role of universities as knowledge transfer or knowledge exchange drivers for the creative and cultural industries is problematic.

Implementing an Agile Helix model offers higher education institutions a means to engage with the creative industries on an infrastructural and human resource level, as well as acting as a collaborative helix facilitator.

This offers the possibility of a helix model that works for and with the creative and cultural sectors and not being distant from it or seen as not applicable. Seeing the university in this role within the Agile Helix also links to the process of creative innovation ecosystem orchestration whereby the university may act not just as an educator but as a civil partner, ecosystem enabler and an anchor in its locality. The concept of the university as anchor institution is well established in both theory and practice for institutions in the developed world, but has, for the reasons noted earlier, yet to be really made concrete in small island states. The Agile Helix model can provide a mechanism whereby local universities or satellite campuses can play a much greater role across social, industrial and cultural communities.

The Agile Helix in SIDS

The challenges for originating innovation in small island states are significant, but implementing an Agile Helix model can greatly increase the collaborative and connected process, enabling all three key actors in the helix to play flexible roles for the benefit of each individual project. To make this happen will require all three actors in the helix to innovate in the way they work with other partners and to recognise the challenges that each faces. Digital, knowledge-based, creative innovation must be seen as just as important as the dominant, but as we've seen, highly vulnerable sectors.

To see how this helix model can work in practice, it is worth examining the role of each player within a SIDS-based Agile Helix.

The role of SIDS universities in the Agile Helix

Universities are highly complex organisations with multiple and often conflicting agendas in a constant state of tension and flux. Their role in local and regional development is gaining greater significance, highlighted by the recent heightened emphasis on civic participation, its impact on regional competitiveness and the support of, or transition to, knowledge-based economies. This often works in tension with the desire to expand their globalised approaches to research and education and the access to student and research finance that they bring. These strategic goals are not mutually exclusive however, and whilst the local and global views often exist in a dialectical tension within higher education institutions, even globally oriented universities can have substantial local and regional innovation impacts (Goddard & Vallance, 2013).

As we've seen, the dilemma for island state universities, with often very limited physical, human and financial resources, is that the imperative to address often pressing local educational needs can negatively impact their ability to be partners and co-producers in the innovation process. The question then is: 'How can universities respond not just to the ever increasing pace of technological change and societal impact but to the continual business model disruption and reconfiguration that industry is dealing with because of these changes and impacts?' The rise of the digital-creative industries as a leading economic force of the twenty-first century is leaving universities and research institutions a long way behind.

Universities have always struggled to engage with the creative sector on a collaborative innovation level, generally seeing their role as a talent pipeline for the industry. The obvious issue with that then is the irrelevance of the Triple Helix model for the creative and cultural industries. If research and innovation in the creative and cultural sectors happens primarily outside the university, then the helix does not exist for these industries in its traditionally theorised form.

Firstly, then, we need to recognise that the traditional helix model is problematic in remote and rural regions such as small island states due to the restricted nature of universities and research capacity. We therefore need to not just develop a new understanding of how these institutions will engage and contribute in the Agile Helix but work to build applied research capability, which is still important for the development of an Agile Helix and successful collaborative and connected innovation. These universities need investment into building applied research centres that relate to the economic development of their regions, particularly around the SDGs but that go beyond the existing developed sectors such as tourism, fisheries and the wider Blue Economy.

Secondly, universities and research organisations need to build new approaches to innovation engagement with the creative and cultural industries beyond simply workforce development. The Agile Helix model frees universities from the KT role of the traditional helix and allows them use all their resources, both physical and human, as part of a flexible innovation flow.

Much of the usual restricted role is seated in the way that universities have seen themselves and have been seen by society and industry. Universities have always been seen as the generators of research and new knowledge, but in the era of ubiquitous social networks and user-generated content, the ability to drive innovation, research and new knowledge outside the walls of higher education has arrived. Universities have singularly failed to respond in any meaningful way to that disruption.

In the same way that the entertainment industry was disrupted by the impact of cheap production and distribution technologies, digital cameras and smartphones for photography and filmmaking, aligned with free global distribution platforms such as Facebook and YouTube, the ability to conduct user-generated and funded research that is then distributed freely and rapidly is impacting the helix model of innovation.

Indeed, as Arnkil et al. (2010) suggest, this era of top-down, expert-driven development is giving way to a more collaborative, connected and community-based innovation. Crowdfunded and crowdsourced research has become more widespread with greater ease of implementation and many SMEs and entrepreneurs are seeing the value of working with academics outside of the restrictions and long lead times of university departments and research council norms. Remodelling the helix to take into account these more dynamic and flexible R&D practices is important if we want to look at how the developing world and small island states can build their own strong and sustainable connected innovation systems.

We still see, however, many recently published research papers expounding the value of KT in language that seems increasingly outdated and irrelevant in the real world. It also still seemingly holds currency among researchers and academics despite a number of studies (Asheim & Coenen, 2005; Kenney & Mowery, 2014; Lawler, 2011) that suggest that this KT model is not delivering on its economic potential and in fact adds to the disconnect between universities and industry through the internalisation of that knowledge.

The addition of a fourth element to the helix, that of civil society or community, to make a quadruple helix is generally put forward as a counter to this problem of disconnected and isolated knowledge (Carayannis & Campbell, 2012), yet if the university–industry–government core of the helix is not revisited and the process by which that research and knowledge creation process is defined and actioned in the initial stages, then the problem still largely remains.

Continuing to add additional elements to the Triple Helix, seemingly ad nauseam, does nothing to address the fundamental challenges with the core of the helix.

We saw earlier how creative and cultural industry practitioners and MSMEs can have a fluid relationship with universities, with personnel often working between the two. Whilst the creative output from these individuals and companies is generally not classed as innovation, we can see these creatives in terms of the soft innovation we discussed. This process can also be seen as a form of reverse knowledge transfer, often discussed in relation to multinational corporations and their subsidiaries (Millar & Choi, 2009).

That is where the role of the Triple Helix and our understanding of the nature and dynamics of the helix need to be reconfigured. This is not a knowledge transfer, or even a knowledge exchange, but a knowledge and innovation co-creation, driven by bi-directional flows. We might see the role of the university here then not as a supplier of new knowledge but as a convenor, facilitator and co-producer. Whilst it therefore diminishes the role of traditional research, it emphasises the importance of human resource and connected, collaborative soft innovation.

Interestingly, it may be that higher education institutions in small islands states may be best placed to implement the disruptive model of the Agile Helix. They are generally smaller, with less historical and academic baggage to negotiate, have a closer and truer community bond and are not encumbered by multiple layers of management and competing faculties in the same way that large institutions in the developed world are.

Introducing the Agile Helix here then may be a first step in not only creating the right environment for island-based innovation but also moving away from the restrictive language and outdated methodologies that characterise traditional KT across the wider Academy.

SIDS universities can do the following then to help make this happen:

a) They can become physical hubs for establishing industry clusters. The distributed campuses of universities such as the University of the West Indies provide a starting point for the implementation of the moveable and mobile hubs discussed in the chapter on clusters.
b) They need to encourage academic staff to become active early stage pro bono advisers to the private sector in SIDS, which often struggles with developing support and mentoring structures.
c) Universities in these regions can encourage entrepreneurs into the academic process, as co-creators of applied research, building the whole creative and entrepreneurial ecosystem.
d) They must enable innovation activity and recognition beyond the boundaries of science and technology so that the digital-creative and knowledge-based sectors can benefit from this co-created innovation flow.

e)   Finally, they can support flexible incubation and accelerator schemes in part-
     nership with the private sector. These do not have to be along the lines of the
     traditional accelerator but can be more flexible in terms of output and process
     to suit the needs and resources of the community.

The role of industry in the Agile Helix

The aforementioned points all place the private sector as an integral part of the
role and activity of universities in SIDS regions. This is important as there is a
noticeable disparity in the agility of actors in a helix, with universities and government often significantly slower to respond to challenges and opportunities
than the private sector. That disparity is also reflected in the research around
the role of industry in the triple, or expanded, helix. Whilst there is a mountain
of literature on the role of universities in the helix and also some considerable
literature on the policy impacts on the Triple Helix, the role of industry and
how the application of the helix to commercialisation plays out are less well
covered.

   This may be due to the traditional primacy of the university in the helix, built
around the concept of knowledge transfer, or a lack of understanding and experience of the real commercial world that can be applied to its research. In the Agile
Helix, the role of industry is just as important as that of research institutions, so
understanding that role and setting out its parameters for driving innovation and
economic development in SIDS are essential.

   Industry must play a leading role in this and not just leave this conceptualisa-
tion to the Academy. Industry therefore needs to take three key steps if they are
to play a truly co-creational role in Agile Helix innovation in SIDS. This is true
across the board, not just of the creative and cultural industries.

a)   Recognise the value of co-creation, innovation and research with other actors
     in the helix. Industry often has a healthy, perhaps well-founded, scepticism of
     higher education and government, but in delivering the benefits of the Agile
     Helix, a truly open and connected approach by all helix actors is essential.
b)   It is vital for the private sector to collaborate in cross-sector innovation, rec-
     ognising the value of cross-disciplinary research and innovation. The ability
     of all industry sectors in small island states to support and collaborate with
     each other is a significant part of building a broad-based, sustainable econ-
     omy. This has often not been the case in the past, so action to reach out to all
     sectors is important.
c)   The creative and cultural industries need to understand and implement greater
     commercial accountability and to build business models beyond a reliance
     on public funding. It is also important for these sectors to decouple creative
     industries growth from cultural heritage. Although it can play a significant
     part of the growth of CCIs in small island states, as we've discussed else-
     where, creative industries are far more than just the exploitation of tangible
     and intangible heritage.

The digital technologies of content creation and distribution offer opportunities for island-based creative SMEs to scale far beyond the limitations of cultural heritage–based commerce.

The role of government in the Agile Helix

The role of government in the Agile Helix is closely linked to its ability to align strategic priorities and tactical decision-making to the needs of the private sector and the input of universities into that process. The restrictions on SIDS governments to act in an agile manner often relate to the challenges of delivering public services across their geographies. Recent research (Everest-Phillips & Henry, 2018) shows that SIDS governments invest a considerable proportion of their GDP to this delivery and that in many SIDS the public sector is the main employer, compensating in some way for the small private sector (Hassall, 2018). Greater use of e-government, as has been demonstrated to some degree of success in the Seychelles, can go some way to not only making this service delivery most cost-effective but also engage greater percentages of the population (Commonwealth Secretariat, 2016).

These public service innovations are essential if island governments are to play a full part in the Agile Helix. It allows greater investment of human and fiscal resource to supporting innovation across the private and public sectors, but particularly in the digital-creative and knowledge-based sectors, ones which have seen little real investment from SIDS governments that have previously prioritised Blue Economy industries.

The important distinction to be made here, and reiterating one made in previous chapters, is that the creative industries, particularly those enabled by digital technologies, are distinct from the concept of cultural heritage. Whilst this cultural heritage, both tangible and intangible, is a vital part of a thriving creative economy, heritage is primarily seen as the responsibility of government to support and fund. The problem with this, of course, is that, as we've seen from previous national and global economic recessions, the arts, culture and creative sectors tend to be the first to suffer from public spending cuts when governments need to save money.

In this instance, reframing SIDS governments as enablers of creative economy development, rather than funders, is central to making that Agile Helix deliverable in these regions. That might not be a popular approach for arts sectors that struggle to be sustainable in such regions, but for long-term development and success, it is essential.

The role of government then in an Agile Helix in any SIDS nation is both a progressive policy maker and an active facilitator and agent. It requires specific, tailor-made policies to foster this kind of collaboration as well as promoting creative ecosystems that are truly sustainable. Whilst an engaged and responsive set of government policies are important at both the local and national levels, this has to be about facilitating and modernising business environments as much as it is about funding. This comes down to assessing and supporting the creative economy in the same way as other industrial sectors, whilst recognising that it has significant spillover and cross-sector value for collaborative innovation.

An example of a successful government intervention is the publication of the UK government's Sector Deal for the creative industries, launched in 2018, which saw a commitment to invest £150 million, jointly by government and industry, into growing the creative economy, supporting the next generation of creative entrepreneurs and widening the creative sector base across the UK (DCMS, 2018).

Whilst SIDS will not have the level of public finance available for such investment in the creative and cultural industries, particularly in the years immediately after the 2020 pandemic and its huge impact on island GDP, the principle of central policy strategy, co-financing strategies and action to enable a more supportive and frictionless business environment are all elements that SIDS governments can action as part of an Agile Helix.

Making the Agile Helix a reality for small island states

The importance of this discussion is not in the proposal of a new theoretical helixical model but in finding an actionable framework for how industry, education and government in SIDS can work in a flexible, adaptive and agile partnership for the benefit of its people.

The importance of the theoretical model is that it shows a way forward for these regions that the more traditional Triple Helix, and its ad nauseam extensions, simply does not cater for. In particular, and given the circumstances of the recovery from the Covid-19 pandemic, the role that international finance, in terms of development banks, venture capital and angel investment, can have in the Agile Helix for small island states cannot be overemphasised.

Investment into universities and research centres as part of that greater link to finance and the finance community, linked to applied research and collaborative innovation as part of a recognised Agile Helix innovation structure, can then drive that all-important indigenous digital-creative and knowledge-based entrepreneurship.

The role of international organisations in realising the value of the Agile Helix concept is also essential, recognising that it provides an island-based mechanism for collaborative and connected island innovation and sustainable economic development. It is an enabler of locally based research, development and solutions to challenges such as the Blue Economy, environmental degradation and social and cultural growth.

Conclusion

Island-based innovation is a topic that is largely missing from research into SIDS, but if the last 12 months have highlighted anything, it is the need to build greater strength in digital-creative and knowledge-based innovation in the regions to broaden their economic bases and help offset the challenges that global events can have on tourism.

Delivering the benefits of the Agile Helix in SIDS will require the integration of the dispersed cluster and moveable hubs models outlined in the last chapter. The social and economic connective tissues that these models enable are vital for engaging and serving the dispersed and poly-centric communities characteristic of so many SIDS populations. It allows all island peoples, not just those in the capital cities or on the most inhabited islands, to have an opportunity to contribute to the success of their communities and to connect with, and benefit from, the strength that a successful Agile Helix can deliver.

References

Arnkil, R., Jarvensivu, A. & Piirainen, T. 2010. *Exploring the Triple Helix: Outlining User-Oriented Innovation Models*. University of Tampere, Institute for Social Research, Tampere.

Asheim, B.T. & Coenen, L. 2005. Knowledge Bases and Regional Innovation Systems: Comparing Nordic Clusters. *Research Policy*, 34(8), pp. 1173–1190.

Brand, M., Tiberius, V., Bican, P.M., et al. 2019. Agility as an Innovation Driver: Towards an Agile Front End of Innovation Framework. *Review of Management Science,* November, pp. 1–31.

Carayannis, E.G. & Campbell, D.F. 2012. Mode 3 Knowledge Production in Quadruple Helix Innovation Systems. In *Mode 3 Knowledge Production in Quadruple Helix Innovation Systems*, pp. 1–63. Springer, New York.

Cavallini, S., Soldi, R., Friedl, J. & Volpe, M. 2016. Using the Quadruple Helix Approach to Accelerate the Transfer of Research and Innovation Results to Regional Growth. Technical Report for European Union Committee of the Regions. EU.

Commonwealth Secretariat. 2016. *Global Youth Development Index Report*. Commonwealth Secretariat, London.

Crespi, G., Fernandez-Arias, E. & Stein, E. 2014. Investing in Ideas: Policies to Foster Innovation. In *Rethinking Productive Development*, pp. 61–106. Palgrave Macmillan, New York.

Crossick, G. 2006. *Knowledge Transfer Without Widgets: The Challenge of the Creative Economy: A Lecture to the Royal Society of Arts*. Goldsmiths, University of London, London.

Cruz, A.R., Almeida, R.N., Costa, P., Gato, M.A. & Perestrelo, M. 2019. Knowledge Transfer in the Cultural and Creative Sector: Institutional Aspects and Perspectives from Actors in Selected Atlantic Regions. *Social Sciences*, 8(3), p. 77.

Department of Culture Media and Sport (DCMS). 2018. *Industrial Strategy: Creative Industries Sector Deal*. DCMS, London.

Drucker, J. & Goldstein, H. 2007. Assessing the Regional Economic Development Impacts of Universities: A Review of Current Approaches. *International Regional Science Review*, 30(1), pp. 20–46.

Dzisah, J. & Etzkowitz, H. 2008. Triple Helix Circulation: The Heart of Innovation and Development. *International Journal of Technology Management and Sustainable Development*, 7(2), pp. 101–115.

Etzkowitz, H. & Leyesdorff, L. 1995. The Triple Helix – University-Industry-Government Relations: A Laboratory for Knowledge Based Economic Development. *EASST Review*, 14(1), pp. 14–19.

Everest-Phillips, M. & Henry, S. 2018. Public Administration in Small and Very Small States: How Does Smallness Affect Governance? *International Journal of Civil Service Reform and Practice*, 3(2).

Fernandez-Esquinas, M. & Pinto, H. 2014. The Role of Universities in Urban Regeneration: Reframing the Analytical Approach. *European Planning Studies*, 22(7), pp. 1462–1483.

Gault, F. 2010. *Innovation Strategies for a Global Economy*. International Development Research Centre, Canada.

Goddard, J.B. & Vallance, P. 2013. *The University and the City*. Routledge, London.

Granger, R.C. 2018. *Alternative Ecosystems in Creative Cities: The Role of Universities and Quintuple Helixes in Crowded Creative Ecosystems*. DeMontfort University. Accessed at http://hdl.handle.net/2086/16314.

Granger, R.C. & Hamilton, C. 2010. Re-Spatializing the Creative Industries: A Relational Examination of Underground Scenes, and Professional and Organizational Lock-in. *Creative Industries Journal*, 3(1), pp. 47–60.

Grundel, I. & Dahlstrom, M. 2016. A Quadruple and Quintuple Helix Approach to Regional Innovation Systems in the Transformation to a Forestry-Based Bioeconomy. *Journal of the Knowledge Economy*, 7(4), pp. 963–983.

Hassall, G. 2018. Special Issue on Public Sector Enhancement in Pacific Island States. *Asia Pacific Journal of Public Administration*, 40(4), pp. 207–211.

Heidemann Lassen, A., McKelvey, M. & Ljungberg, D. 2018. Knowledge-Intensive Entrepreneurship in Manufacturing and Creative Industries: Same, Same, but Different. *Creativity and Innovation Management*, 27, pp. 284–294.

Jeannerat, H. & Crevoiser, O. 2016. From 'Territorial Innovation Models' to 'Territorial Knowledge Dynamics': On the Learning Value of a New Concept in Regional Studies. *Regional Studies*, 50(2), pp. 185–188.

Kenney, M. & Mowery, D.C. (Eds.). 2014. *Public Universities and Regional Growth: Insights from the University of California*. Stanford University Press, Stanford, CA.

Kolehmainen, J., Irvine, J., Stewart, L., et al. 2016. Quadruple Helix, Innovation and the Knowledge-Based Development: Lessons from Remote, Rural and Less-Favoured Regions. *Journal of the Knowledge Economy*, 7, pp. 23–42.

Lawler, C. 2011. The Capitalisation of Knowledge: A Triple Helix of University-Industry-Government. *Studies in Higher Education*, 36(6), pp. 746–747.

Miles, I. & Green, L. 2008. *Hidden Innovation in the Creative Industries*. Project Report, NESTA. Manchester Metropolitan University, Manchester.

Millar, C. & Choi, C. 2009. Reverse Knowledge and Technology Transfer: Imbalances Caused by Cognitive Barriers in Asymmetric Relationships. *International Journal of Technology Management*, 48(3).

Muller, K., Rammer, C. & Truby, J. 2009. The Role of Creative Industries in Industrial Innovation. *Innovation*, 11(2), pp. 148–168.

Navarro, J.C., Benavente, J.M. & Crespi, G. 2016. *The New Imperative of Innovation: Policy Perspectives for Latin America and He Caribbean*. Inter-American Development Bank. Accessed at https://publications.iadb.org/en/handle/11319/7417.

Rigby, D., Sutherland, J. & Takeuchi, H. 2016. Embracing Agile. *Harvard Business Review*, May.

Stoneman, P. 2010. *Soft Innovation: Economics, Product Aesthetics, and the Creative Industries*. Oxford University Press, Oxford.

Viale, R. & Campodall'Orto, S. 2002. An Evolutionary Triple Helix to Strengthen Academy-Industry Relations: Suggestions from European Regions. *Science and Public Policy*, 29(3), pp. 154–168.

6   Ecosystems and orchestrators

Introduction

Small Island Developing States are well versed in the concept of ecosystems, particularly those of the oceans. Just as fragile and dynamic, though, are the economic and innovation ecosystems that are in such urgent need of development in these regions. The disruption that is occurring in global markets through the accelerating impacts of the 4IR, not to mention the devastating effects of the Covid-19 pandemic, is seeing many traditional companies and sectors struggling to adapt and survive. Like the negative impacts on those fragile natural environments, the ecosystems of commerce and innovation are under pressure like never before.

In the face of these challenges, the need for positive and rapid transformations, by both private companies in their operations and strategies and government departments charged with responding to national and international economic pressures, is more important than ever. Key to these micro- and macro-level adaptations is the ability to connect and collaborate in product and process innovation, through the ecosystems of development, production and distribution. These ecosystems have been recognised for some time within industrial strategies, often with the concept of clusters at its heart, as we saw in the earlier chapter.

The new models of dispersed clusters and moveable hubs for SIDS have to also move beyond the norms of cluster activity, looking instead to orchestrating and leading the development of complete ecosystems. When assembled and nurtured effectively, these ecosystems can address issues that lie beyond the capabilities of any one entity – whether that be an SME, local government, Chamber of Commerce or any other support network. They can also do this in ways that are faster, cheaper and more user-friendly than alternative approaches.

These business ecosystems are nothing new but are usually described either in terms of supply and distribution chains or, as discussed previously, in terms of Triple Helix innovation networks. The ecosystems required over the next five to ten years are wider, more complex and more dynamic. They include the education and skills pipeline, targeted R&D collaborations, start-up support, and access to finance so that successful start-ups can scale and cluster organisations that can be the framework in which all of these elements can sit effectively and efficiently.

By bringing together various players and groups with distinct strengths, a successful ecosystem is able to capture new value, set the stage for innovation, develop and scale solutions, improve customer loyalty and create sustainable revenue streams. Of course, that is easier said than done. However, the reformulation of the Triple Helix into an Agile Helix provides a mechanism whereby the connectivity and innovation potential of that agile system can be orchestrated by new model clusters to form an effective and highly responsive ecosystem.

The concept of ecosystems

It was British botanist Arthur Tansley (1935), who first coined the term 'ecosystem' to describe the interaction of organisations with each other and their environments. Sixty years later Moore (1993) adopted this term to describe how the increasingly interconnected world of business replicated that natural world in terms of companies interacting with multiple suppliers, partners and physical distribution systems, what Moore called the 'organisms of the business world'.

The term is often used as a metaphor, using the competitive, symbiotic and environmental relationships of the natural world as a descriptor for the similar workings and dynamics of the business world. This then finds a related use as an organisational strategy for business and regional economic development (Anggraeni et al., 2007).

In the creative and cultural industries, the term has been used to describe how this sector's complex set of relationships, collaborations and transactions was important to regional economies (Jeffcutt, 2004), and this regional approach has been taken on by Bakalli (2014), who looks at creative ecosystems from a European perspective and in a number of reports on the UK creative economy from NESTA (2008, 2013, 2018).

In much the same way then that the Triple Helix needed to be reconceptualised into the Agile Helix to enable it to work with different geographies and different parameters, a similar approach to ecosystem development and sustainability needs to be implemented so that the constraints of previous models do not impinge on the opportunities and needs of regions such as those with SIDS.

Business ecosystems

Ecosystem is an almost ubiquitous word when regional business and economic development concepts are being discussed. It is used to frame many discussions, theories and strategies, from start-up and entrepreneurial networks, to clusters, finance and markets.

The concept of business ecosystems was introduced by Moore (1993), who defines a business ecosystem as an economic community that exists to support value creation and competitive advantage. As such, this concept is a way of rethinking organisational strategy, growth and competition. He saw the business ecosystem as a way of facilitating the bringing to market of monetiseable innovations, rather than just process improvement (Moore, 1996). This concept also draws upon the natural world metaphor by stressing the importance of the overall health of the ecosystem to each of the individual actors within it (Anggraeni et al., 2007; Moore, 1996). Just as in the natural world, business ecosystems are a complex and highly dynamic set of economic, innovation and human interdependencies that whilst seeming to be successful and stable are, like biological systems, subject to considerable stresses and vulnerabilities.

Whilst this concept provides a useful mechanism for describing how companies and organisations operate, trade and collaborate in their value chains, Moore's model does focus on larger companies and fails to take into account the way medium, small and micro-businesses are created and developed.

For ecosystems in SIDS this is a critical point as many firms, particularly in the digital-creative and cultural sectors, are micro or small- and medium-sized companies (MSME). This exclusion is addressed in the work by Isenberg (2011), who focused on entrepreneurial innovation within a regional context and approached it from an economic perspective.

Entrepreneurial ecosystems

Isenberg describes the entrepreneur as someone who looks to create growth through economic value and a dissatisfaction with the status quo (Isenberg, 2011). He then outlines the six domains of the entrepreneurial ecosystem as:

1 **Policy**
   This includes the regulatory framework put in place by governments such as taxation and tax incentives, intellectual property rights, labour markets and regulations and R&D.

2 **Finance**
   A crucial element for entrepreneurship and this domain is centred around access and levels of micro-loans, venture capital, angel investors, private equity and public capital markets.

3 **Culture**
   Social norms around creativity, the status of entrepreneurs, tolerance of risk, wealth creation and international reputation.

4 **Supports**
   This broad domain includes physical and digital infrastructure such as transport, ICT and energy, along with the quality and specialisms of professional services.

5 **Human Capital**
   A key element for growth is the access to skilled and unskilled labour, the education pipeline of universities and the level of continuing professional and vocational education.

6 **Markets**
   These are both domestic and international markets and market access, along with knowledge of customers and demographics.

This ecosystem description has commonality with creative businesses and creative business models (Bilton, 2006), emphasising as it does the pursuit or new value through innovative thinking, production and distribution. This model also highlights the issues faced by small island states in building a viable economic innovation ecosystem, with every domain described seeing significant challenges for these regions.

Isenberg's model is not sector-specific and is a similar broad-brush approach to that of the later entrepreneurial ecosystem model put forward by the World Economic Forum (WEF, 2013). The WEF report highlights the importance of three main pillars for entrepreneurial ecosystem success, these being accessible markets, human capital/workforce and funding and finance. It also highlights that whilst the issues facing entrepreneurs around the globe show a large degree of commonality, the variance of localised ecosystems across the main issues is often substantial. This has particular relevance to developing and small economies where many challenges and barriers exist and programmes of development to address these barriers are often siloed, disjointed or sector-specific.

Knowledge ecosystems

We saw in the previous chapter that the positioning of universities as the prime driver in Triple Helix relations no longer particularly holds true, especially for the digital-creative and cultural industries. Alongside this and as we've seen in other instances, the literature can be slow to recognise this shift with research still citing the importance of universities and research institutions to innovation and start-up activity (Link & Scott, 2013; Lofsten & Lindelof, 2001). The main argument here is that the flow of tacit knowledge from universities to industry and then the resulting flow between companies in a particular sector, aligned with the mobility and influx of talent that universities facilitate (Saxenian, 1996, 2006), drive the creative of innovation hotspots and ecosystems.

This set of relationships have been termed Knowledge Ecosystems, mirroring the structure of the traditional Triple Helix, placing universities and research organisations at the centre of a system that drives primarily advanced technological innovation. The problem with emphasising the primacy of universities and research institutions in either innovation and knowledge ecosystems or industry–university–government helixical relationships is the inflexibility of those models for the 'other geographies' discussed in the earlier chapter on clusters, especially for SIDS with both small urban centres and limited higher education capacity and resource.

In reframing knowledge ecosystems then, the term has to be freed from its coupling to university research so that a more contemporary understanding of knowledge production and dissemination can be applied. This reframing will help address the difficulties discussed in the previous chapter of seeing university knowledge transfer or knowledge exchange in the creative and cultural industries. This can incorporate the concept of user-generated knowledge where online communities can participate in open and collaborative innovation (Ye et al., 2016) and, particularly in the creative and cultural industries, the informal networks and collaborations of micro and small enterprises in discrete projects.

Creative ecosystems

Creative ecosystems provide an interesting example of ecosystem development and growth as they combine business, knowledge and entrepreneurial systems in an inter-relational network that often steps outside the norms of traditional models. Much of the literature that describes these creative ecosystems often cite the importance of close public–private sector relationships and the link of these relationships to local communities. Collaborative development and the interdependence of these diverse actors are seen as central to these ecosystems and the strategies devised for their success (Bakalli, 2014).

The social, commercial and innovation networks that constitute creative clusters, whether organic or established as a formal initiative, are the most usual examples of creative ecosystems. These local or regional creative ecosystems often closely engage with national agencies such as Arts Councils, Government Ministries of Culture and cultural diplomacy NGOs. The intervention of government in these creative ecosystems is largely unique to the creative and cultural industries, given their perceived status as drivers of social cohesion, identity and education on both national and local levels (Heilbrun & Gray, 2001).

Because of this role, regional or city-based creative ecosystems often have strong connections to local communities, the corollary of this understanding then being the continued relevance, despite the rise of virtual networks and production, of co-location to the creative process and creative entrepreneurship. Given this, the importance of the creative cluster and the creative city to the success and sustainability of the creative ecosystem then seems obvious (NESTA, 2013).

In 2014, the United Nations Industrial Development Organisation (UNIDO) highlighted the role of creative clusters as a vehicle to develop creative economies, as well seeing the Triple Helix as a vital player in these economies (Bakalli, 2014. The Creative Ecosystem: Facilitating the Development of Creative Industries. UNIDO, Geneva).

What may be seen as lacking in that report is the recognition that the reality of its application on the ground in many developing regions makes establishing creative clusters challenging and makes Triple Helix dynamics without a university with established research resources almost irrelevant, and that the lack of suitable population size of many urban centres in regions such as those of SIDS makes the classic 'creative city' model almost impossible.

Previous chapters have shown though that rethinking these concepts, such as those of the creative cluster, will enable a more applicable and inclusive approach to developing creative ecosystems in challenging regions such as small island states. The benefits of some level of physical co-location, of creative entrepreneurs coming together to share knowledge and experiences, are not in dispute. It is the reality of its facilitation that requires rethinking, which is why the conceptualising of the dispersed cluster and the moveable or mobile hub can become the model by which creative ecosystems thrive in SIDS.

The creative city as ecosystem

The manufacturing and value production mechanisms of cities have evolved over the last 50 years and in particular since the creative industries revolution of the 1990s. In his book *The Cultural Economy of Cities*, Scott (2000) outlines the key features and challenges of urban economies that moved from an economy based on material value production to one of immaterial value. He defined this new city economy as a cognitive-cultural economy, one based on technology-intensive production and services, creativity, culture and design.

This concept of the creative city grew out of the economic crisis of the 1970s, a period that saw the difficult transition from the post-war manufacturing boom in urban economies to a smaller scale, fragmented and growing service-sector orientation. That process saw huge social disruption, urban decay and economic stagnation in many cities and regions of the developed world. The loss of physical manufacturing saw the rise in the importance of an economy based on immaterial value and a new route to urban regeneration for national and city region governments.

The creative and cultural industries proved to be the foundation on which to build that regeneration and the 'creative city' became not just an accepted and widely replicated model of urban development and redevelopment but the means by which cities could brand and promote themselves in an increasingly competitive global investment, talent and tourism landscape (D'Ovidio, 2016).

The locating of creative and cultural individuals in cities of course is nothing new. Artists and musicians have migrated to cities in search of benefactors and clients for as long as cities have existed. What has changed over the last 30 or so years is the rise of these sectors as a global economic force, beyond that of the individual.

The city is seen as the natural home for these sectors as they represent the right conditions for creative innovation to thrive. The model is familiar and applied to the point of ubiquity. The concentration of people allows sectors and specialisms to mix, triggering innovation. Bars and coffee shops become the meeting ground for creatives and innovators to meet, share experiences and knowledge, and form collaborative projects. The vibrant mix of diverse peoples and ideas spawn new practices, concepts and outputs. Creative businesses are close to clients, to investors and to a constant inflow of new opportunities for work. The economic, cultural and social ecosystems of urban centres then are perfectly suited to the development and growth of creative and cultural SMEs.

But therein lies the problem.

The use of the creative and cultural industries to drive urban regeneration became so strategically systemic that the notion of creative economies has become completely synonymous with cities. Separating the two so that the benefits of creative economy development can be made more spatially, socially and culturally even requires not just theoretical innovation but a recognition by governments and international organisations that the creative and cultural industries can have a leading role to play in sustainable, knowledge-based economies globally, even in SIDS, which seem on the face of it, to be the antithesis of the 'creative city'.

The role of government in creative ecosystems

The impact of the creative and cultural industries on urban regeneration then has cemented their importance as a sector for support and intervention for governments. It has also been recognised that the outputs of the sector, in terms of goods and services, have significant social, cultural and educational value as well as economic ones (Frey, 2000), and therefore it is important to make such goods and services as widely accessible as possible through financial support and subsidy.

Whilst these roles remain, the emphasis is changing. The rise of 'creative economies' as a concept, the recognition of its growing importance in global trade, facilitated by the digital technologies of production, distribution and consumption, and the increasing participation of the world's population in those technologies have all altered the dynamic of government intervention.

Whilst the social aspects of creative economy outputs still hold true, the emphasis has turned to growing and support economic ecosystems as an important driver of high-value, high-skill jobs, export revenue and local economic growth. This then feeds into the second area of government intervention, based around the particular cost and value chain structures of the creative industries that see high initial input costs, such as in the production of film and television content, followed by marginal costs that can be low (Caves, 2000).

The argument was that this economic structure generates barriers to entry, allowing established companies to take advantage of their market position, resulting in high levels of market concentration and monopoly which could adversely impact consumers and attempted new entrants. Intervention was required then to address these possible monopolies and to incentivise new products and firms through financial and taxation instruments (Newsinger & Presence, 2018).

This argument however has been losing relevance for some time as the opportunities for production, distribution and monetisation become more and more widely available. Technology costs have dropped dramatically, making production now far more democratised. Mobile devices now have the capability to record in 4K and offer cheap, transportable means of recording and editing. Other similar arguments revolved around the barriers associated with distribution channels. Broadcasting, for example, traditionally involved similar high sunk costs to film and television production and thus allowed the creation, again, of natural monopolies (Towse, 2010).

Once again though, this is no longer the case. The rapid development of streaming technologies, cheaper broadband with greater capacity and more reliability, along with mobile reception and distribution has seen the creation of Over the Top Television (OTT), allowing content producers to stream long-form drama, documentary and news programme to an audience with vastly reduced costs in terms of both the producers and the consumers and bypassing, or going 'over-the-top' of, traditional broadcasters altogether. Sites like YouTube now stream live operatic performances for free, allowing consumers access to cultural production on a whole new scale. These new technologies around streaming, OTT television, the role out of 5G test beds and the rapidly falling costs on all sides can be truly transformational for small island states and developing regions as a whole, negating the argument around high initial costs and a barrier for low-income consumers.

For example, at the start of the 2010s, Myanmar had rates of mobile and internet penetration that were comparable to North Korea. In 2014, the government opened up the telecommunications market, and within three years there were more active SIM cards in the country than people, having the highest rate of smartphone penetration of any developing country (Heijmans, 2017). To put this in context, Myanmar has an annual income per capita of US$1,245 and 24.8% of the country's 53.71 million people live near or below the poverty line (World Bank, 2020). All this is not to say that government support for CCIs is not important, but it has to be recognised that the mechanisms, needs and barriers must be carefully assessed using contemporary industry data before such interventions are prioritised and publicly funded.

The role of the Agile Helix

If these interventions are to be effective in building and sustaining creative economy ecosystems, then this has to be done as a public–private partnership, engaging all the key regional and national players. However, ecosystems are highly variable, so entrusting too closely to a fixed model can often be detrimental to its creation and orchestration (Furr & Shipilov, 2018). The spatial geography of the region or country, the political and regulatory environment, the dominant industries already there and the level of competition all impact on the strategic approach to either creating or sustaining an ecosystem. This is where the Agile Helix can play such an important role, taking into account local or regional needs and environments and responding quickly and efficiently to changes and challenges.

Nurse (2017), in his work on the creative and cultural industries in the Caribbean, makes an important point around the need for enabling institutions for creative economies in SIDS as a way to support the growth and industrial upgrading of the sector. The key lesson he points to though is that most existing institutions operate in silos with limited linkages to other initiatives or programmes.

This is not restricted to the Caribbean region and can be seen in many other SIDS regions as well as other developing countries. The issue then is to find the mechanism whereby these institutions, organisations and supporting actors can communicate and collaborate so that the creative sector works not in isolation but is able to build a complete ecosystem that intersects with and draws upon the support of the wider commercial, financial and legal frameworks. The linkages that help build and then support this ecosystem can be delivered through the flexible structures of the Agile Helix, outlined in the previous chapter. It allows the combining of knowledge ecosystems and business ecosystems into a single system, ameliorating the negative effects of isolation that Nurse (2017) points out.

This Agile Helix can then work in partnership with the new models of clusters and hubs, described in the previous chapter, to create the mechanisms whereby these delicate ecosystems can be managed and orchestrated.

Orchestrating ecosystems

Creative ecosystems tend to be seen as naturally occurring in developed regions and more specifically in cities and large urban centres. The preponderance of 'creative city' papers, projects, hubs, clusters and funding all point to the fact that it is the combination of the geographical, human and fiscal environment that makes these locations most obviously suited to creative ecosystem growth. The Centre for Cities makes the important point that because cities are a mix of a broad range of sectors, they aren't often considered as clusters.

But this is one of their key strengths. Particular industries do cluster within cities, and the importance of links within sectors is likely to explain why we see this clustering. For example, in central London law clusters around Chancery Lane, finance concentrates in the City and advertising has made its home in Soho.

But by co-locating with other industries, the potential arises for innovation to occur across sectors as well as within, and this is what cities offer that single industry clusters do not, access to other companies in both the same and other sectors. So the argument that the Centre for Cities makes is that it is cities that are important, not clusters (Centre for Cities, 2017).

One would expect this argument from an organisation with such a title, and although one can see some logic in this approach, it is a rather limited and reductionist approach. It may work for cities, but for regions around the world that do not possess these large urban areas and the density they provide, this approach is flawed at best and at worst exclusionary. Unfortunately, this simple linking of creative economies to cities is seen not just in theoretical studies but in major organisations and is even stated explicitly as fact. UNESCO (2013), for example, states that a creative economy consists of a cultural and creative industry located in creative cities.

In a global economy where the drive, quite rightly, is for greater equity and inclusion, whole regions and countries simply cannot be ignored because they don't fit a perceived theoretical model or where creative economy growth and innovation are challenging and difficult to achieve. This is not to argue against the premise that cities offer positive environments for creative innovation to flourish, which is unquestionably true, but the case has to be made for resources, research and investment to also be put into the development of innovation infrastructures in other regions and particularly in SIDS, however hard that might be. If we don't, then we relegate these countries to being simply the recipient of the developed world's activity and creativity. We see this already in the approach to climate change and the environment projects and research, something that is all too often 'done to' rather than 'done with' SIDS regions.

We risk perpetuating the semi-colonial approach discussed in Chapter 2 if we don't work in complete collaboration with countries and regions to develop creative, knowledge-based, innovative and sustainable economies.

Unfortunately, the overwhelming priority given to research and funding around innovation in cities assumes that it can only happen in cities and areas of population density. Whilst this certainly may be an important driver of creative activity and creative innovation, not looking at how the tools, methods and learning around creative innovation can be used in other regions and geographies only exacerbates the unevenness of development – within developed countries and even more noticeably between developed and developing regions (Huggins & Thompson, 2014).

We've seen the issues that can be caused by this lack of development spread. If the SDGs are to be achieved, then innovation and creative networks in these regions have to be given a chance to seed and thrive. The challenge of achieving this in small island states is even more significant but no less important. In fact, it takes on an even greater importance as the accelerating degradation of ocean environments and the negative impacts of Covid-19 on the tourist economy become clear. It requires a remodelling of the creative ecosystem concept, one that works for small island states, rather than an acceptance that creative ecosystems as a whole are not applicable to the particular spatial and economic characteristics of SIDS.

An ecosystem for SIDS

For SIDS, any concept of a workable creative and entrepreneurial ecosystem seems especially problematic. Creative ecosystems include such a broad set of actors that the commercial, collaborative and knowledge exchange relationships and interactions often lack the formal structures of other sectors, and as such the ability to create this in dispersed geographies such as SIDS seems unlikely. A different mechanism then is required from the traditional creative cluster or creative city approach, one where SIDS can first build and then successfully orchestrate digital-creative ecosystems for their regions and locally based entrepreneurs.

Using cluster initiatives to turn the creative city into the creative island

If the 'creative city' does provide the best environment for creative economy development, then for SIDS, which lack the urban density and associated close connections between actors normally required for that approach, it presents a significant problem. Another way forward needs to be found, and this may be taking the key outputs from the creative city and remodelling them into an actionable strategy for these regions – turning the 'creative city' concept into the new 'creative island'.

We saw from the case study of the Platform creative cluster in Chapter 4 that the principles of the creative city can be extracted and delivered through the model of a Dispersed Cluster (Rudge, 2016). The particular poly-centric nature of the city region that Platform works in presents many of the same geographical challenges as SIDS regions like the Eastern Caribbean or archipelagic nations like the Maldives. This cluster initiative can then act as an orchestrator for the creative ecosystem in small island states. Whilst ecosystems in large urban centres can function and thrive organically, for developing regions and smaller population areas, the ecosystem requires an active orchestrator. This orchestration is focused on identifying and engaging the key partners and stakeholders, ensuring the outreach of activity to all parts of the population, on driving the vision for the creative ecosystem and on making sure that policy, finance and skills development are all aligned (Rudge, 2010).

The Centre for Cities proposed the defining of a creative city as a creative cluster, seeing the activities and connections of the city as similar to those of the creative cluster. As a route to finding an ecosystem methodology then for SIDS, the experience of the Platform cluster suggests perhaps the reverse could also work, that seeing a managed creative cluster initiative as a form of creative city enables all the benefits of urban centres to be replicated through the activities of a Dispersed Cluster.

Using this cluster mechanism and the associated mobile or moveable hubs allows dispersed or rural populations to connect to the ecosystem, to develop a more inclusive approach to the creative economy and to allow an increased innovation and talent pipeline to be developed. The role of clusters as orchestrators of an ecosystem of creative production and investment can take the place of the more organic mechanisms that play out in large urban environments. As such then, it is important to see a collaborative strategic vision in place to develop these cluster initiatives, one that brings the key industry, government and educational stakeholders together with external and international partners. The best method of achieving and then managing these relationships is through the Agile Helix.

Using the Agile Helix to support the creative island ecosystem

The value of the Agile Helix is that it responds both to the highly dynamic nature of the digital-creative industries and to the uncertainties of national and international economic environment caused by the Fourth Industrial Revolution and other external shocks.

This flexible nature also makes it particularly appropriate for developing helixical relationships in SIDS, where the traditional Triple Helix may struggle to work effectively due to the limited human and physical resources of many island universities.

This is not to say however that the higher education system in many SIDS regions does not require investment, quite the reverse. It is essential to develop higher education capabilities in island nations, in terms of both creative and digital research activities and the expertise to deliver high-quality teaching in these vital areas. That then feeds into that managed ecosystem enabled by the creative cluster and facilitating the connected and collaborative innovation that cities take for granted.

The ability of the Agile Helix to move beyond the primacy of the university allows other players to support and take the leading roles as necessary in collaborative creation and innovation, therefore giving the education system of SIDS the breathing space not only to grow teaching and research activity but to input into the helix as a facilitator of the cluster orchestration process.

So the cluster as orchestrator, linked to an Agile Helix, can effectively become the 'city'. The moveable and mobile 'hubs', outlined in Chapter 4, then give the mechanisms whereby the connective relationships found in cities and city districts can be replicated across the dispersed and polycentric populations in small island states.

These mobile hubs though need to operate in a different way if they are to facilitate the 'cluster as city' concept. Although they have proved effective and are still seen as a central part of many strategic growth plans for creative economies, hubs tend to be passive, relying on their positioning within often already well-established creative and cultural environments, or as part of a determined growth plan for a city district, Birmingham's development of the Custard Factory in Digbeth being a good example of this.

The moveable hubs in SIDS in contrast need to be, by definition, active, taking on the role of incepting as well as supporting creative and collaborative innovation. It is this active role that can support the cluster initiative and the Agile Helix in replicating the social, economic, educational and creative innovation fabric that defines the success of the 'creative city'.

Government interventions for the creative island ecosystem

Whilst preserving, celebrating and monetising island cultures, both tangible and intangible are recognised and accepted recipients of government interventions; as we discussed earlier, the role of government more widely in the creative and cultural industries is being reshaped by technology. The fact that digital technologies now allow creative content producers to access huge global markets from anywhere in the world with a fast internet connection means that the digital-creative industries now require a different approach from governments to that of the usual 'subsidise and socialise'.

For small island states whose governments struggle to manage the delivery of basic services alongside the impact of economic uncertainty and external shocks, investment into 'the arts' is often a low priority. However, there are interventions that island governments can make that do not require substantial public investment.

In seeking to support a creative island economy then, there are three key areas that SIDS governments need to address:

a) Create a better private sector business and investment environment. Access to government-backed debt finance, along with policies to establish special economic zones (SEZs) and start-up support infrastructure, will help local entrepreneurs to establish and then scale digital-creative businesses.

These policies enable entrepreneurs to effectively and cost-efficiently locate their business on islands and to remain there as they grow. The strength of the local government support for entrepreneurship then builds confidence in external financial markets to invest in these creative entrepreneurs. The Maldives government's decision to establish seven enterprise centres across the archipelago to support private sector entrepreneurship is a positive example of such an early stage intervention.

b)   Gather contemporary, relevant and high-quality research data on the digital-creative sectors. The importance of data in strategic decision-making for companies is clear, as is its economic value. For governments as well, data on the economic performance of their countries is important for policy making. Yet all too often, and especially in developing regions, data on the creative industries is either incomplete, out of data or is simply not collected at all at any significant granular level (Bakshi, 2014).

Supporting the growth of creative industries research at SIDS universities and within the private sector then enables the gathering of local, reliable data on these sectors to assist in the policy making and strategic development process. As part of the Agile Helix, this government partnership with island universities and entrepreneurs offers the possibility of greater resource into applied academic research and the support and engagement of industry in that process.

c)   Implement robust legislative frameworks for intellectual property rights. This is vital in giving companies the confidence to produce content that can be sufficiently monetised within their local and regional markets. For example, interviews with producers conducted in the Eastern Caribbean as part of the research for this book highlighted an issue where local TV stations often play copyrighted material acquisitions, from either their own islands or elsewhere, without paying the necessary rights fees.

This example of insufficient or unenforced IPR regulations results in a lack of revenue that can be invested back into the content industry. Government intervention here then is particularly important as situations like this not only impact the revenues that producers receive but also inhibit external investment into the sector. These interventions are essentially focused on legislative rather than financial support and can provide a relatively simple first step in creating the right conditions for digital-creative ecosystems to develop and thrive.

Conclusion

The challenges of establishing and then orchestrating creative ecosystems in SIDS are not easily overcome. Innovation will be required from all parties in the way that these challenges are approached, in the models and methods used and, perhaps crucially, in the perceptions of the role that the digital-creative industries can play.

The SDGs and the huge challenge posed by the 'Decade of Action' highlight the flexible, collaborative and connected thinking that the skills, assets and expertise of creative ecosystems can offer (WEF, 2019). In light of that, progress towards and the ultimate realisation of that 'Decade of Action' will only be achieved if strong digital-creative ecosystems can be implemented not just in SIDS but across the developing world.

For SIDS, the lack of population density and the difficulties that arise from that in terms of building a creative economy ecosystem that encapsulates collaborative innovation, creative knowledge exchange and targeted investment are undeniable, as we've discussed here and in previous chapters. There has often been an approach to this from many national and international organisations that border on a metaphorical shrug of the shoulders, followed by a chorus of comments that whilst outwardly positive, in practice, actually amount to little more than a resigned 'oh well'.

The huge negative impact of the Covid-19 pandemic has shown just how vulnerable these island states are to narrow economies and an over-reliance on traditional industries. I include the sectors of the Blue Economy in that description. The need to build the right conditions for other sustainable and high-value industries for these regions is now urgent, and the creative ecosystem must sit at the top of that list.

The ability of the Agile Helix to build this ecosystem and then to use the mechanisms of the dispersed cluster and moveable hubs to make them sustainable presents a compelling case for a way forward, a way to build the creative islands that can address this and the other pressing development needs of SIDS. This however requires all the local and regional stakeholders and institutions to engage and embed with the ecosystem, its cluster orchestrator and its constituent entrepreneurs; otherwise, the co-created value of such an ecosystem can be lost.

The temptation of national or regional governments and institutions may be however, given the challenges of creative economy development in SIDS, to rely on a top-down approach to supporting ecosystems that are already in place and mature, rather than recognising the value of alternative and high-growth sectors (Gaughan et al., 2018).

To guard against this, effective advocacy and leadership is essential, not only to engage these institutions in dialogue around creative ecosystem development, but also to push for research, data gathering and partnerships with existing international creative economy leaders. This can then assist national governments and regional institutions in assessing the best use of limited resources, both financial and human, in supporting this development.

Just as in the oceans that surround them, the creative economy ecosystems of SIDS are fragile, diverse and easily destroyed. By employing the models and mechanisms described in this chapter, we can ensure that they grow and thrive for future island generations.

References

Anggraeni, E., Den Hartigh, E. & Zegveld, M. 2007. Business Ecosystems as a Perspective for Studying the Relations between Firms and Their Business Networks. ECCON 2007 Annual Meeting, pp. 1–28, Netherlands.

Bakalli. 2014. *The Creative Ecosystem: Facilitating the Development of Creative Industries*. UNIDO, Geneva.

Bakshi, H. 2014. *Measuring the Creative Industries*. NESTA, London.

Bilton, C. 2006. *Management and Creativity: From Creative Industries to Creative Management*. Oxford Blackwell, Oxford.

Caves, R.E. 2000. *Creative Industries: Contracts Between Art and Commerce*. Harvard University Press, Cambridge, MA.

Centre for Cities. 2017. *How Do We Encourage Innovation Through Clusters?* London. Accessed at https://centreforcities.org/publication/encourage-innovation-clusters.

D'Ovidio, M. 2016. *The Creative City Does Not Exist: Critical Essays on the Creative and Cultural Economy of Cities*. Ledi Publishing, Milan, Italy.

Frey, B.S. 2000. *Arts and Economics*. Springer, New York.

Furr, N. & Shipilov, A. 2018. Building the Right Ecosystem for Innovation. *MIT Sloan Management Review*, 59(4), pp. 59–64.

Gaughan, P.H., Javalgi, R.G. & Young, R.B. 2018. An Institutional Theory Approach to Improve Planning for Innovation and Entrepreneurship Ecosystems in Developing Economies. *KnE Social Sciences*, pp. 122–130.

Heilbrun, J. & Gray, C.M. 2001. *The Economics of Art and Culture*. Cambridge University Press, Cambridge.

Heijmans, P. 2017. The Unprecedented Explosion of Smartphones in Myanmar. *Bloomberg Businessweek*.

Huggins, R. & Thompson, P. 2014. Culture, Entrepreneurship and Uneven Development: A Spatial Analysis. *Entrepreneurship and Regional Development*, 26(9–10), pp. 726–752.

Isenberg, D. 2011. The Entrepreneurial Ecosystem as a New Paradigm for Economic Policy: Principles for Cultivating Entrepreneurship. Presentation at the Institute of International and European Affairs, Dublin, Ireland, May 12.

Jeffcutt, P. 2004. Knowledge Relationships and Transactions in a Cultural Economy: Analysing the Creative Industries Ecosystem. *Media International Australia Incorporating Culture and Policy*, 112(1), pp. 67–82.

Link, A. & Scott, J. 2013. US Science Parks: The Diffusion of an Innovation and Its Effects on the Academic Missions of Universities. *International Journal of Industrial Organisation*, 21(9), pp. 1323–1356.

Lofsten, H. & Lindelof, P. 2001. Science Parks in Sweden: Industrial Renewal and Development? *R&D Management*, 31(3), pp. 309–322.

Moore, J.F. 1993. A New Ecology of Competition. *Harvard Business Review*, 71(3), pp. 75–86.

Moore, J.F. 1996. *The Death of Competition: Leadership & Strategy in the Age of Business Ecosystems*. Harper Business, New York.

NESTA. 2008. *Hidden Innovation in the Creative Industries: Research Report*. NESTA, London.

NESTA. 2013. *A Manifesto for the Creative Economy*. NESTA, London.

NESTA. 2018. *Creative Nation: How the Creative Industries Are Powering the UK's Nations and Regions*. NESTA, London.

Newsinger, J. & Presence, S. 2018. United Kingdom: Film Funding, the "Corporate Welfare System" and Its Discontents. In *Handbook of State Aid for Film*, pp. 447–462. Springer, Cham.

Nurse, K. 2017. The Creative (Orange) Economy and the Caribbean: How to Promote Creative Entrepreneurship and Move Up Global Value Chains. Presentation to the Orange Economy Webinar, Creative Nassau, Nassau.

Rudge, P. 2010. *Developing the Screen Industries in North Staffordshire. Report for the North Staffordshire Regeneration Partnership.* Stoke on Trent, UK. Accessed at http://eprints.staffs.ac.uk/5084

Rudge, P. 2016. *A Framework Strategy for the Stoke on Trent and Staffordshire Moving Image Cluster.* Stoke on Trent and Staffordshire Local Enterprise Partnership, UK. Accessed at http://eprints.staffs.ac.uk/3741

Saxenian, A.L. 1996. *Regional Advantage: Culture and Competition in Silicon Valley and Route 128.* Harvard University Press, Cambridge, MA.

Saxenian, A.L. 2006. *The New Argonauts: Regional Advantage in a Global Economy.* Harvard University Press, Cambridge, MA.

Scott, A.J. 2000. *The Cultural Economy of Cities: Essays on the Geography of Image-Producing Industries.* Sage Publishing, Thousand Oaks, CA.

Tansley, A.G. 1935. The Use and Abuse of Vegetational Concepts and Terms. *Ecology*, 16(3), pp. 284–307.

Towse, R. 2010. *A Textbook of Cultural Economies.* Cambridge University Press, Cambridge.

United Nations Educational Scientific and Cultural Organization. 2013. *Creative Economy Report 2013 Special Edition. Widening Local Development Pathways.* UNESCO, New York.

World Bank Myanmar Data. 2020. Washington, DC. Accessed at data.worldbank.org/country/Myanmar.

World Economic Forum. 2013. Entrepreneurial Ecosystems Around the Globe and Company Growth Dynamics. Report Summary for the Annual meeting of the New Champions, 2013. WEF, Geneva.

World Economic Forum. 2019. *Platforms and Ecosystems: Enabling the Digital Economy.* Briefing Paper. WEF, Geneva.

Ye, J., Blohm, I., Breschneider, U., Goswami, S., Leimeister, J.M. & Krcmar, H. 2016. Promoting the Quality of User Generated Ideas in Online Innovation Communities: A Knowledge Collaboration Perspective. 37th International Conference on Information Systems, 2016. Dublin, Ireland.

7 Creative entrepreneurship and inclusive innovation

Introduction

The purpose of establishing the strong and sustainable creative ecosystems described in the last chapter is to energise and support creative entrepreneurship. The challenges of achieving this in SIDS, whilst undeniably significant, are not insurmountable, particularly if we also apply the concept of innovation and entrepreneurship to the policies and practices of supporting these activities. All too often we've seen the strategies to support innovation inherently lacking the very characteristics they want to build. Alongside this is the essential drive to be more diverse and inclusive being built on concepts that are exclusionary and homogeneous. More often than not this is not a deliberate act but a failure to think innovatively about what innovation and entrepreneurship is.

If SIDS are to build the digital, creative and knowledge-based economies that are now so essential to their future sustainability, then the way innovation and entrepreneurship is supported and financed in these regions has to be innovative in itself, not built on restrictive practices and concepts.

The concept of entrepreneurship

Innovation and entrepreneurship are inherently creative activities, regardless of the sectors involved or the outputs achieved. The conceptualising of something new and the vision and imagination to step beyond the normal bounds of a product or service are what mark the entrepreneur from simply the business owner. Entrepreneurs are agents of change, driven by the recognition of a problem that in turn creates a commercial opportunity. Over the last 30 years, the term has become ubiquitous, entering popular culture as a signifier of creative ambition, wealth creation and status. It is also now recognised as an essential part of every country's economy as a creator of new jobs and prosperity (Galindo-Martin & Mendez-Picazo, 2020).

Because of this, the concept of entrepreneurship has seen its cultural and social value rise, with increasingly knowledge-based economies linking creative and entrepreneurial skills ever more closely, with the status and social capital of the entrepreneur as celebrity continuing to rise.

This creative entrepreneurship has also become more visible with the increasingly rapid pace in technological and product development cycles that has seen the lifetime of products falling ever more quickly. This then has the knock-on effect of making large product standardisation and production less important. Creativity, innovation and rapid response times are the new central tenets of commerce.

Innovation is also becoming increasingly open with creative and cultural entrepreneurs forming collaborative working partnerships to bring sectors and knowledge together. The impact of these economic and technological developments are putting severe strain on social, ethical and governance frameworks that also then, in turn, require creative, entrepreneurial innovations to address them.

There are, however, complex and often ingrained issues with developing these entrepreneurial innovation ecosystems. Organisations and governments at a local, national and international level are struggling to see their policies and strategies keep pace with economic and social changes, leading to a mismatch between appropriate structural and fiscal support frameworks. This is evident in the dogmatic coupling of innovation to science and technology in many research, policy and strategy documents.

Policy and strategy are also struggling to address the widening spatial inequalities in entrepreneurship and innovation. This is true with developed economies and is multiplied many times over in developing countries and island states. These regions are often rural or semi-rural in nature, feature small or dispersed populations or are polycentric in terms of urban concentrations. The focus on cities as centres of creative innovation and entrepreneurship still persists despite many declarations to make economic participation and development more equal.

The challenges of achieving this goal for developing regions are hindered by their ability to respond to externally caused recessions like the financial crash of 2008 and the even greater recession caused by the Covid-19 pandemic of 2020. According to Mitra (2019), this is where entrepreneurship can really succeed, in distressing circumstances that require new ideas, new structures and new approaches – necessity indeed being the mother of invention.

Entrepreneurship is however high-risk, with failure rates, even those tech-based, venture capital backed start-ups, hitting more than 90% (Gauthier & Penzel, 2020). To enable these start-ups to innovate and then move beyond the seed phase and into revenue and growth, access to finance, mentoring and business support across the whole development spectrum becomes essential.

Innovation beyond science and technology

The narrative of innovation is linked almost exclusively to science and technology, in terms of research, government reports, policies and strategies. There is a perception that the creative and cultural industries create but don't innovate.

NESTA has done some outstanding work here in promoting a more inclusive approach to innovation policy and understanding, but there are also some problematic areas in these reports. The report on inclusive innovation in ASEAN countries (Glennie et al., 2020) produced in conjunction with the OECD puts forward some strong and well-reasoned arguments around innovation for social inclusion but fails to discuss moving innovation beyond the perception of innovation being solely driven by science and technology. This seems to be in contrast to their own report of 2008 on the importance of soft innovation.

Innovation in the creative and cultural sectors is one of the most important drivers of social and economic inclusion, enabling more young people and women to access and engage in entrepreneurial activity. Any discussion then of inclusive innovation has to see those sectors as central to their argument, particularly in the developing regions of the Global South.

Hartley et al. (2019) highlight how the role of low-technology innovation in developing countries is undervalued in addressing global challenges by the dominant assumption that high-technology innovation is the primary driver of economic development. This is despite all the evidence for soft innovation and value creation in the creative and cultural sectors and the economic performance of these sectors globally.

Many similar reports and research papers fail to see that responsible and inclusive innovation is about not just opening up innovation to a wider section of society but also seeing it as part of every sector and driven by more than just widgets and software. When this limited approach is picked up by governments and translated into policy, it becomes actively exclusive. Fiscal instruments, investor perceptions and restricted research focus then follow, leading to a narrowing of the innovation base and a lag on economic, social and cultural entrepreneurialism.

Governments can innovate in how they support creative economies, entrepreneurialism and innovation. Business groups can innovate in how they approach the whole commercial process, the 'B Team', for example, being a group of industry leaders who are looking to innovate in process, inclusion and sustainability, taking a very different approach to how this can be done.

Unfortunately, these aspects rarely get discussed in research and reports into innovation methods, policy or application. In the post-Covid-19 world though, there needs to be a drive to innovate in a responsible and inclusive manner that engages not just science and technology but soft, creative and cultural innovation, an approach that is particularly important and relevant now to developing regions and small island states. That responsible innovation is based on the engagement of stakeholders across business, society and community to solve the key social and environmental challenges highlighted in the sustainable development goals.

Soft innovation and the impact of CCIs on entrepreneurship

The impact that the creative industries have had on entrepreneurship has been substantial in terms of the approach to innovation and innovation leadership. The recognition within industry of the value of the creative industries as a route to building corporate and intellectual property value has transformed the creative and cultural sector. This, in combination with the ubiquity of cheap digital technologies in production and distribution, has seen the CCIs become the most dynamic global sector for economic growth.

Soft innovation is becoming more and more important as creative and cultural sector business models and social structures change. This is more than just the aesthetic innovation of new books, films, fashions and music, for example. Soft innovation today also encompasses service and business models, social frameworks and network development.

The two of course are inextricably linked, technology driving creative and cultural creation, innovation and service change, whilst creative disruption often leads to the necessity of delivering changes and innovations in technology and science. The merging of the digital content and digital platform industries is a good example of this connected, hybrid innovation, a merging of the aesthetic and the technical, driven by entrepreneurs, communities and creators.

NESTA produced an important report on this back in 2009 (NESTA, 2009), yet the uptake and understanding of the value of soft innovation still seem to be lost on many organisations, government departments and research funders. This results in innovation still being closely linked textually with science and technology, which then impacts on the approach to supporting and delivering innovation activities in the real world.

The perception and use of the term 'R&D' also falls into this misconception. The majority of definitions of R&D focus on the scientific and technological aspects of the activity and is particularly important if an entrepreneur or SME is looking to access government R&D tax credits, for example. The official definition in these documents then tends to exclude arts, creative and cultural statements, which not only makes it difficult for companies to access funding and tax incentives for these activities but also calls into question the accuracy of national and sub-national R&D activity data, as the metrics used are then by their very nature limited and limiting. Given that the service sectors are now the largest, or one of the largest sectors of many economies, the lack of policy literature on soft innovation is surprising (NESTA, 2009).

Disruption is often seen as a technology-driven action, yet, as the NESTA report points out, the business model innovation that led to the creation of low-cost airlines was a highly significant and far-reaching disruptive soft innovation, as was Uber and Airbnb. This soft innovation is important for universities to understand as well, as it impacts how they develop and implement strategies for the support and engagement with knowledge exchange outside the traditional technical and technological faculties. The need for this conceptual redefinition highlights the importance of moving from triple/quadruple helix models to the Agile Helix.

This realisation of the value of this soft innovation is central to how the relationship between creative industries and entrepreneurship has changed over the last 30 years, giving rise to the global creative economies in the context of what Scott (2010) calls cognitive cultural capitalism. This idea, as a post-Fordist concept, seeks to describe the knowledge-based economies of the late twentieth and now twenty-first centuries. Nowhere was the emergence of this new economy more evident perhaps than in the work done by the UK Government of Tony Blair in the late 1990s to establish the 'creative industries' concept and the branding of 'Cool Britannia'. This was made concrete in the mapping document produced by the Department for Culture, Media and Sport (DCMS) in 1998, one of the most important policy documents in the history of the creative and cultural industries (Gross, 2020).

The UK Government's decision to establish a Creative Industries Task Force in 1997 that led to the mapping document reinforces Scott's argument (2010) that creativity and creative production could be seen as a social phenomenon closely aligned to the various and interlinked social relationships that enable it. Central to this is the notion that creativity is intrinsically tied to place and more importantly, as we've seen previously, to urban places, in what is described as the 'urban creative field'.

This concept has had considerable influence on how and where creative entrepreneurs work and the infrastructural, policy and strategic development that allows them to collaborate and innovate. Co-working spaces, hubs and clusters have seen cities as their natural home, and this is understandable given the collaborative nature of creative and cultural production, along with the dynamic social, cultural and intellectual spaces of the city.

Chapter 4, 'Clusters beyond the city', discussed the changing spatial landscape of creative and cultural industry economics, with many capital and tier-two cities starting to see the negative impacts of rapid urban growth in traffic congestion, the high cost of land, increasingly marginalised populations and an increasing level of infrastructural deterioration. In this instance the development of smaller cities, towns and even rural regions offers the possibility of creating strong entrepreneurial communities that can act as engines for their regions, promoting then a more even, polycentric and inclusive development.

Crucially, the digital-creative sector is dismantling the notion of creative industries and creative entrepreneurship being tied primarily to cities, place and cultural heritage. The Covid-19 pandemic of 2020 led to a surge in remote working technology implementation, as well as investment into new real-time, geo-dispersed, collaborative creative production in fields such as visual effects and animation.

The social element that Scott describes as central to the creative process is, thanks to technological development, becoming more and more dispersed and virtual. Whilst collaboration and creative connectedness is undoubtedly central still to the creative industries, the process by which this happens and the locations in which it happens are changing. This has the possibility to allow entrepreneurs in the rural, remote and developing regions such as SIDS to be part of creative industry production, connecting to and developing projects and new ventures, accessing work and finance, and facilitating a more even and inclusive creative sector – across both the Global North and Global South.

This greater access to and inclusion in the creative and cultural industries for dispersed populations have significant impacts for SIDS. All too often, island populations are seen as simply workforce for outside innovators in tourism, the

Blue Economy or environmental or clean energy projects, rather than possible innovators themselves. The peoples of these island states are one of its most valuable and most undervalued resources.

They can be a source of innovation, entrepreneurialism, wealth creation and economic transformation if the structures to support them can be put in place. As has been stated previously though, these support structures need innovation in themselves.

The Parliament of the European Union, for example, produces a series of fact sheets on a wide range of policy areas, and its approach to supporting innovation is replicated across many governments and institutions. It recognises the growing importance of innovation to national and global economies, but its description and resultant understanding of innovation is revealing. It describes innovation policy as "the interface between research and technological development policy and industrial policy" (European Union, 2020).

Again, this puts forward a traditional and limited view of what innovation is, tied to research institutions and the production of new science and technology, thereby substantially restricting the impact that a more informed innovation policy could have. If policy is predicated on the perception that innovation is primarily linked to science and technology, then it fails to support the much wider soft innovation occurring in MSMEs across the whole economy and crucially the entrepreneurs engaged in those fields.

For developing regions and small island states, it is vital therefore not to see these policies as exemplars for their own industrial strategies. Rather, they need to respond to the accelerating pace of economic change by supporting entrepreneurial and innovation activity through flexible, responsive, sectorally inclusive strategies that understand the heterogeneous nature of innovation.

We saw from the chapter on the Agile Helix how the relationship of universities, industry and government is changing and how the concept of an Agile Helix allows greater collaborative innovation flow in dynamic systems. In supporting creative entrepreneurialism then in small island states, the old structures and understandings of innovation and entrepreneurship can no longer apply.

The role of education in developing entrepreneurship in SIDS

To make this happen in these developing regions, education has a key role to play. Access to post-secondary education in many SIDS and other developing regions is patchy at best, with most students needing to travel to the main or capital cities to find opportunities to study (UNESCO, 2012). Small states also have distinct needs that relate to their scale, isolation and dependency and are not simply smaller versions of developed countries (Commonwealth Secretariat, 1995). In looking then at how education can play a role in developing an entrepreneurial ecosystem, transferring existing methods from developed and larger countries will not be effective.

Crossley and Sprague (2014) highlight that education will play a central role in reaching the SDGs, particularly in coordination with national and international socio-economic initiatives. This collaborative approach to the SDGs has to take into account the development of island entrepreneurship as a key component of these goals, and education is central to the foundational strength of entrepreneurial ecosystems.

Education for entrepreneurship, not entrepreneurship education

The early work by Jamieson (1984) on entrepreneurship education saw it as a discipline focused on giving students a set of skills, knowledge and attitude that would then allow them to innovate and create value around those innovations.

One could argue that this set of attributes could also be the result of a plethora of other degrees, particularly those in the classic liberal arts fields, areas of study that are now being touted as one of the key drivers of education for the 4IR. Whether one believes that the teaching of entrepreneurship as a distinct set of skills and competencies is possible, or is simply a rebranding of existing approaches and courses, the concept has gained considerable traction. One can see evidence of this in the variety of commercialised proprietary entrepreneurship 'systems' that promise to deliver the best results either in education or in industry.

One might argue then that the best approach for education to take in supporting the growth of entrepreneurship is not to teach entrepreneurship but to concentrate on the broad development of creative, critical and cognitive skills, as the WEF report on the future of work pointed out. So whilst there is little doubt that some of the skills and knowledge that make a successful entrepreneur can be taught, the empirical evidence to link the teaching of entrepreneurship to increased levels of successful start-ups and scale-ups is still missing.

This is distinct from the broad impact that universities can have on social and economic development, with many universities now actively promoting the civic aspect of their research and teaching, what Markuerkiaga et al. (2016) describe as turning the university into an entrepreneurial university. This is based on the ability of staff, students and graduates to commercialise their research through the formation of spin-out companies.

The issue for SIDS is that the level of entrepreneurial activity at island universities is low, being hampered by the resources available to support staff and graduate entrepreneurship and the experience of teaching staff in delivering mentoring and support to any entrepreneurial students. As has been argued earlier, building an entrepreneurial community and ecosystem is not necessarily based on the teaching of entrepreneurship, so in looking at how education, across all levels, can play a part in this for SIDS, it is important to recognise the variables at play in each community or island education establishment.

Kirkley (2017) highlights not only the importance but also the challenges of 'culture' in developing this community. He argues that community culture is central to the role of educators and the education system. The key then in developing entrepreneurial skills and attitudes, in what can be very traditional island communities, is the redefining of education strategies and their relation to all the stakeholders in sustainable development.

The engagement of secondary schools in this process of developing entrepreneurial skills and awareness, particularly in rural communities or in outlying atolls away from capital cities, is as important as that in higher education. It is at the secondary school level that the engagement of young people, particularly young girls, in creative and critical thinking is built. If we want to develop a more inclusive approach to education for entrepreneurship and build the foundations for success at tertiary level and beyond, then the process starts here. Unfortunately, it is not just the current geographical and educational infrastructure of SIDS that is a barrier to this development. International institutions, although providing important financial and technical support for education development, also perpetuate some restrictive concepts and strategies.

The World Bank Enhancing Education Development Project worked with the Government of the Maldives from 2013 to 2018 to assist in addressing the challenges of the education sector in the country. The project had many positive outcomes around improving quality assurance, professional development for teachers and improvements in management systems and data.

However, one of its key reforms, preparing young Maldivians for the local job market, whilst undoubtedly of importance and well intentioned, highlights a narrow approach to the link between education and economic development. The project was focused on job preparedness for the twenty-first century, but in its report on the project (World Bank, 2019), a key aim was stated as being the development of a new curriculum more relevant to the job market and, in particular, the tourism industry. There was no mention of aspiration, of creative and critical thinking and of helping young Maldivians create their own wealth and job opportunities through innovation and entrepreneurship.

In a post-Covid-19 landscape, with the challenges that the tourism sector faced during the pandemic and the ensuing severe economic recession, looking beyond such traditional approaches and engaging young islanders in sectors that can enthuse them and encourage them to enrol in post-secondary education have to be a priority. Educational aspiration and attainment go hand in hand, so looking to a more inclusive, engaged and creative curriculum is essential.

Making entrepreneurship and innovation inclusive

This need for inclusivity is vital if island economies are to recover and become more resistant to economic and other external shocks. This inclusivity may be hindered by national or local culture; as Kirkley (2017) noted, it may be due to geographic restrictions, such as remoteness and difficulties in travel, or it may be a result of inadequate policy interventions at either a national or international level.

Again, NESTA has done some important and insightful work here. Its Inclusive Innovation Policy Framework (Gabriel et al., 2018.) in particular notes the importance of impact as part of policy frameworks and within that the areas that link closely with a number of the key SDG targets such as the environment, health and sustainability. This policy at national level needs to be aligned and coordinated with strategy and funding at international level if inclusive entrepreneurship and innovation are to move forward.

Whilst many national policy interventions exist to enhance inclusivity around gender and race, spatial inclusiveness is somewhat lacking. One can see this in developed countries such as the UK, where there still is a significant economic imbalance between London and the South East and the Midlands and North, despite the declarations of successive governments and initiatives such as start-up support network Tech Nation.

This is also reflected in the research and strategic programmes noted earlier, where regions or geographies are simply not seen as either being fertile-enough ground or having too many challenges for any real interventions around indigenous innovation and entrepreneurship to take hold. Whilst this is never explicitly said, the reality on the ground for these regions is, as we've seen above, very different.

However, a recent jointly published report by NESTA and UNDP (NESTA, 2020) found some interesting and relevant examples of inclusive innovation in the emerging economies of South East Asia, namely Indonesia, Myanmar, the Philippines and Vietnam. Programmes to include a wider variety of groups including women, veterans, people with disabilities and rural communities were all part of government initiatives to spread innovation.

The objective of reaching out to connect the previously unconnected societal groups and communities is an important lesson for SIDS and one which governments and international organisations need to take on board. Regional clusters, outreach programmes, innovation networks outside cities and the implementation of Agile Helix collaborations between industry, universities and governments can translate from these countries to SIDS, despite the increased challenges that these island nations face. This is an approach that NESTA (2020) describes as 'innovation everywhere'.

It is important, however, not to slip back into seeing technology and science as the only mechanisms for spreading innovation but to realise that soft innovation can also be just as important here. What is crucial is the ability to connect digital-creative innovation into every other sector of the economy to enhance the innovation practices and opportunities. There are obvious lessons here for inserting this creative practice into key sectors for SIDS such as tourism and the wider Blue Economy.

The purpose of making innovation and entrepreneurship more inclusive, in all its forms and meanings, must be to enable a greater impact across all sections of society. The aligning of international intervention strategies to this purpose has to be predicated on achieving the SDGs, and nowhere is this more salient than in small island states.

Entrepreneurial ecosystems

If greater inclusion in innovation and entrepreneurship is to be achieved in these island regions, then the nurturing of entrepreneurial ecosystems is the mechanism by which it can happen. We saw in the previous chapter that Isenberg (2011) highlighted how these ecosystems need an environment that is located in a free market, contains liquid capital markets, and has sufficient talent and an entrepreneurial culture.

It is then how all these elements interact and influence each other that defines the success, or otherwise, of an entrepreneurial ecosystem (Spilling, 1996).

We also saw how orchestration is a key part of an ecosystem's success, particularly in those regions where the concentration of actors is lower, in rural, developing or island communities for example, or the cultural infrastructure around innovation and entrepreneurship is not well established. Whilst many of the creative economy ecosystem success factors discussed in the last chapter also apply to entrepreneurial ecosystems, there are some specific elements that allow innovation and entrepreneurship to thrive. In essence, entrepreneurial ecosystems enable the conceptualising of ideas, through a managed innovation and development process to the point at which these can be monetised through the creation of a start-up venture.

Creative economy ecosystems, or wider business systems, are about the growth and sustainability of all the actors within that ecosystem, be they start-ups, scale-ups or long-established companies. So whilst elements such as stable commercial, legal and policy environments, access to suitable debt and equity capital markets and a supply of talent and skills are common to both, unlike the stabilising and long-term economic ecosystem, entrepreneurial ecosystems require the injection of early collaborative ideation, a dynamic and socially capitalised culture and targeted policy and fiscal tools.

They also include some specific actions and activities around creative innovation, its support and the move from product concept to commercial reality. The connection of innovation hubs and clusters to the specifics of start-up accelerators is a well-worn path for city governments, regional development agencies and universities. The ability to 'hothouse' pre-start-up teams, develop minimum viable products (MVPs), test concepts and products through early and rapid prototypes and then link this to expert mentoring and, finally, seed investment is a well-proven model for entrepreneurial support (Cohen et al., 2019: Gebczynska & Kwiotkowska, 2019).

In creating similar entrepreneurship programmes in SIDS, the same innovative approaches as those highlighted in the conceptualising of the Agile Helix and the decentralised cluster model need to be applied.

Building entrepreneurial islands

What we've seen in previous chapters is that the traditional perceptions of island economies, their vulnerabilities and their opportunities are in need of change and innovation. Whilst this is happening in some areas, the old modalities are hard to shake off.

Underpinning the future success of sustainable SIDS economies are the people of these islands. Despite the understandable concentration of island governments and international development agencies on areas such as tourism and the wider Blue Economy, the greatest resource of small island states is the creativity, ingenuity and culture of the indigenous population. In building innovation and entrepreneurship in the regions then, giving people the tools and knowledge to take charge of their own future has to be a key priority.

What perhaps is not recognised is that the opportunities for island entrepreneurs are now greater than ever, with future innovation and entrepreneurship in these regions being driven by a number of positive factors.

The digital technologies of the Third and now Fourth Industrial Revolutions open up routes to markets that have never existed before for SIDS. Digital platforms, content, products and artefacts all have the potential to reach global audiences and consumers from anywhere in the world. The isolation of these communities from traditional trade routes that were for so long a limiting factor on island-based entrepreneurs is now no longer the case. The opportunities then for island entrepreneurs to attract finance for their ventures are greater than ever, with investors able to see the possible returns available through these new creative technologies.

A factor in the ability of entrepreneurs in developing regions to attract finance is the rise of impact investing, something that has been growing substantially in the last decade. In 2010, less than $3 trillion of investments were made into companies having environmental, social and governance factors as part of the decision-making process. By 2018 that figure was over $12 trillion, driven by growth of the 'conscious consumer' and the financial success achieved by companies that respond to that consumer (US Sustainable Investment Forum, 2018).

Socially conscious millennial investors are now a significant factor in the flow of international impact investment and by 2025 will make up around 75% of the US workforce. Their consumer behaviour has driven the transformation of the retail market, and this behaviour is now feeding through into the investment industry as that demographic becomes wealthier. Indeed, globally this generation is projected to be the richest ever, with an estimated inheritance windfall from their 'baby boomer' parents of around $68 trillion over the next 25 years (USSIF, 2018).

Whilst these factors all point to a significant opportunity for entrepreneurs in SIDS, and although impact investment has increased in developing regions, the level of non-debt investment into start-up and scale-up companies in these regions remains low. This is often driven by perceptions, sometimes accurate, of difficult legal and business environments in these countries along with insufficient stability in political systems (OECD, 2019).

The OECD (2019), whilst highlighting the importance of these international impact investors, rightly points to the role that local investors need to make in these regions. It stresses the role that this international finance must play in the development of a strong local financial market, able to create intermediaries that can engage these local investors and so build the financial infrastructure that so often deters international angel and VC investors.

In looking at the mechanisms then to finance island entrepreneurship, work needs to be done to build the ecosystem that sits around the investment instruments, so that both entrepreneurs and investors have the confidence to enter into collaborative innovation and development.

Financing island entrepreneurship

The ability of island states to develop and grow their entrepreneurial culture and output rests on a number of pillars, but no doubt central to all this is the access to suitable finance for private sector R&D and innovation.

It is also important to see this investment in light of the drive to implement the 2030 Agenda and the challenges of engaging entrepreneurship and the whole private sector in that process. Many of the challenges are real, such as increasing the ease of doing business in many developing countries, improving and implementing intellectual property rights legislation, and building the educational and research infrastructure of innovation and entrepreneurship. There are however competing perceptions around the role of the private sector in the SDGs and economic development as a whole that cloud the key issues and hinder the rapid progress that is required.

Whilst many governments and some international organisations recognise that sustainable development cannot happen without the support and engagement of the private sector finance, some, such as many NGOs and academic researchers, see the dangers of private sector profit and wealth generation at the expense of the poorest countries (Abshagen et al., 2018). Unfortunately, this misunderstands the dynamic between top-down policy and agenda setting and bottom-up delivery and implementation.

Whilst governments and international organisations can set the broad agenda, engage multiple partners in strategy development and encourage nations to set policy interventions, the long-term sustainable implementation of the SDGs lies in the hands of the private sector in partnership with the public sector.

This is particularly true of the private investment community, as simply basing SDG finance on shifting a percentage of global GDP is unrealistic. To make that happen however, to encourage a shift in capital allocation to SDG-aligned investments, requires governments to remove the constraints to capital supply and to incentivise private sector finance into these sectors.

The OECD (2016) set out some broad principles for engaging the private sector in development cooperation, with the basis of leveraging the financial, technical, innovation and research capabilities of the private sector, whilst recognising its need for a financial return. This is important not just in terms of the large multinational companies that are often engaged in development projects but in every aspect of the private sector.

This will then widen the approach to targeting development capital, understanding that the 2030 Agenda is going to be delivered not simply through the funding of large-scale, infrastructural investment but also by the engagement of MSMEs in that process. Finding mechanisms for this, such as the implementation of blockchain-based technologies and smart contracts within a suitable policy framework, can ease the restraints that entrepreneurs in SIDS or other developing regions face in attracting and accessing seed, start-up and scale-up finance.

Beyond finance though, MSMEs in SIDS and developing regions contribute to sustainable development through the positive impact of innovation and commercial activity in their localities. Building local production and inserting this into regional and global value chains contributes to the ability of these communities to become sustainable. This collective effort, of governments, development organisations and the whole range of the private sector, is essential if the 'Decade of Delivery' is to have any chance of being realised.

An important step in this public–private cooperation is the adoption of the Kampala Principles at the meeting of the Steering Committee of the Global Partnership for Effective Development Co-operation (GPEDC) in Kampala in 2019. It set out five key principles for making these partnerships as effective and impactful as possible (GPEDC, 2019).

1   There is a need to strengthen coordination, alignment and capacity-building at a country level, thereby delivering greater inclusive country ownership.
2   These partnerships need to show real results and targeted impact on the group, and this is a mutually beneficial process.
3   Partnerships need to be built upon trust, dialogue and inclusiveness if they are to deliver the required impact.
4   Projects and partnerships need to be transparent and accountable, with mechanisms for gathering data, measuring the outputs and impacts and then disseminating these for further projects.
5   That no-one is left behind and that all partners recognise, share and then mitigate risks for each other.

The importance of these principles lies in the recognition of the heterogeneity and diversity of the private sector and that country level ownership is important if the ecosystems of entrepreneurship and innovation in developing regions are to be nurtured to contribute to sustainable development. Whilst there are notable challenges in implementing these principles, particularly around compliance, multi-country ownership guidelines and IP legal frameworks, the framework itself provides a useful roadmap in guiding the creation of such partnerships and ultimately of building island entrepreneurship.

Conclusion

Sustainable development can be defined as meeting the social and economic needs of the current generation without damaging the ability of future generations to do the same. It is about raising the standard of level for everyone now and in the future. For SIDS that balance is a hard one to achieve and is often impinged upon by external climate and economic factors. That being the case then, taking as much of that sustainable development action into one's own hands has to be the way forward and creating an innovative, entrepreneurial and economically active island population is the way to achieve that. As we've seen in previous chapters, the digital-creative industries provide the mechanisms to make that a reality.

This, however, will require some notable changes in thinking, particularly by governments and international development organisations that perhaps still see island entrepreneurship as secondary to large-scale internationally driven infrastructural interventions.

There are positive actions though that are already happening on the ground. Seedstars is an organisation that supports start-ups and entrepreneurs in developing regions and has been active in the Caribbean and the Maldives, with competitions, mentoring programmes and access to investors for these emerging markets.

The YHER Pacific Islands Programme supports early stage female entrepreneurs in the Pacific region with access to funding, skills and knowledge development and community networks. It is also now being rolled out to African countries.

These examples of positive action need to be supported by national governments to make them sustainable and more impactful, as well as by the research community to gather data that can be used for dissemination and learning. The danger is that they remain isolated and always working with limited resources.

The metanarrative of vulnerability and the tunnel vision approach to certain industry sectors have the potential to limit the success of sustainable economic development in small island states. What can challenge and overcome those limited views are the innovation and entrepreneurship of island peoples that ultimately build the opportunities for a strong creative future.

References

Abshagen, M-L., Cavazzini, A., Graen, L. & Obenland, W. 2018. *Hijacking the SDGs? The Private Sector and the Sustainable Development Goals*. Report for the German NGO Forum on Financing for Development, Berlin.

Cohen, S., Fehder, D.C., Hochberg, Y.V. & Murray, F. 2019. The Design of Startup Accelerators. *Research Policy*, 48(7), pp. 1781–1797.

Commonwealth Secretariat. 1995. *Vulnerability: Small States in the Global Society*. Commonwealth Secretariat, London.

Crossley, M. & Sprague, T. 2014. Education for Sustainable Development: Implications for Small Island Developing States (SIDS). *International Journal of Educational Development*, 35, pp. 86–95.

European Union. 2020. *Innovation Policy Factsheets*. EU, Brussels. Accessed at www.europarl.europa.eu/factsheets.

Gabriel, M., Glennie, A. & Stanley, I. 2018. *How Inclusive Is Innovation Policy?* NESTA, London. Accessed at www.nesta.org.uk/report/how-inclusive-innovation-policy.

Galindo-Martin, M-A. & Mendez-Picazo, M-T. 2020. Value Creation, Innovation and Entrepreneurship: Feedback Effects. In Galindo-Martin, M.A. (Ed.), *Analysing the Relationship Between Innovation, Value Creation and Entrepreneurship*, pp 1–20. IGI Global, Pennsylvania, PA.

Gauthier, J.F. & Penzel, M. 2020. *The Global Startup Ecosystem Report, 2020*. Startup Genome, San Francisco.

Gebczynska, M. & Kwiotkowska, A. 2019. Role of Accelerators in Development of the Entrepreneurial Ecosystem as a Part of the Regional Economic Development Strategy. In IOP Conference Series. *Materials Science and Engineering*, 471(10).

Glennie, A., Ollard, J., Stanley, I. & Klingler-Vidra, R. 2020. *Strategies for Supporting Inclusive Innovation: Insights from South-East Asia*. NESTA/UNDP, London.

Global Partnership for Effective Development Co-operation. 2019. *Kampala Principles: On Effective Private Sector Engagement in Development Co-operation*. UNDP, New York.

Gross, J. 2020. *The Birth of the Creative Industries: An Oral History of the 1998 DCMS Mapping Document*. Kings College London, London.

Hartley, S., McLeod, C., Clifford, M., Jewitt, S. & Ray, C. 2019. A Retrospective Analysis of Responsible Innovation for Low-Technology in the Global South. *Journal of Responsible Innovation*, 6(2), pp. 143–162.

Isenberg, D. 2011. The Entrepreneurial Ecosystem as a New Paradigm for Economic Policy: Principles for Cultivating Entrepreneurship. Presentation at the Institute of International and European Affairs, Dublin, Ireland, May 12, 2011.

Jamieson, I. 1984. Schools and Enterprise. In Watts, A.G. & Moran, P. (Eds.), *Education for Enterprise*, pp. 19–27. CRAC, Ballinger, Cambridge, MA.

Kirkley, W.W. 2017. Cultivating Entrepreneurial Behaviour: Entrepreneurship Education I Secondary Schools. *Asia Pacific Journal of Innovation and Entrepreneurship*, 11(1), pp. 17–37.

Markuerkiaga, L., Caiazza, R., Igartua, J.I. & Errasti, N. 2016. Factors Fostering Students' Spin-off Firm Formation. *Journal of Management Development*, 35(6), pp. 814–846.

Mitra, J. 2019. *Entrepreneurship, Innovation and Regional Development*. Routledge, London.

NESTA. 2009. *The Innovation Index: Measuring the UK's Investment in Innovation and its Effects*. NESTA, London.

NESTA. 2020. *Strategies for Supporting Inclusive Innovation: Insights from South-East Asia*. NESTA, London.

Organisation for Economic Development and Co-operation. 2016. *Peer Learning: Lessons from DAC members on Effectively Engaging the Private Sector in Development Co-operation*. OCED, Paris.

Organisation for Economic Development and Co-operation. 2019. *Social Impact Investment: The Impact Imperative for Sustainable Development*. OECD, Paris.

Scott, A.J. 2010. Cultural Economy and the Creative Field of the City. *Geografiska Annaler: Series B, Human Geography*, 92(2), pp. 115–130.

Spilling, O.R. 1996. The Entrepreneurial System: On Entrepreneurship in the Context of a Mega-Event. *Journal of Business Research*, 36(1), pp. 91–103.

UNESCO. 2012. *Education for Sustainable Development: Building a Better, Fairer World for the 21st Century*. UNESCO, Paris.

US Sustainable Investment Forum. 2018. *Report on US Sustainable and Impact Investing Trends*. USSIF, Washington, DC.

World Bank. 2019. Preparing Young Maldivians for the Modern Marketplace. Accessed at www.worldbank.org/en/news/feature/2019/09/02.

Conclusion
Creative futures for Small Island Developing States

"We cannot solve our problems with the same thinking we used when we created them."

This quote, attributed perhaps somewhat apocryphally to Albert Einstein, might be the shortest but most accurate response to the challenges we face at the start of the third decade of the twenty-first century.

This book has attempted to apply that concept to the challenges of achieving the SDGs, the impacts and often overlooked opportunities of the creative economy, and how they both apply to building stronger and more resilient SIDS that can look beyond the Blue Economy.

Each of the chapters has examined what I feel are the key components of meeting this challenge, from the new technologies of the 4IR to the educational, financial and policy structures required to support that growth and the collaborative innovations that can come from it. Central to these arguments is the concept of the creative economy not just as an important sector in itself but as a driver of innovation across every other sector. In researching and writing this book, it has become clear that it is not just the 4IR that is driving the transformation of the global economy but a movement that harks back to a revolution from more than six hundred years ago.

2CR: the Second Creative Revolution

Innovation is driven by creative entrepreneurialism, whether that is in immersive technology, tourism, clean energy, healthcare or design. The ability of the digital-creative industries to engage young people in education and then offer them opportunities to build successful knowledge-based businesses means that the entrepreneurial, start-up and creative ecosystem grows and impacts across the whole of economy and society. The World Economic Forum produced a report entitled *The Future of Jobs* (World Economic Forum, 2018) in which they concluded that the most important skills for the new landscape of the 4IR were creativity, critical thinking and complex problem-solving. Many technology leaders are now talking about the central role that liberal arts education and not necessarily STEM, or even STEAM, graduates will have in the development, design and implementation of this new industrial and societal landscape.

Digital transformation is a well-used phrase to describe the process of how these new technologies can be beneficially implemented across business systems, governmental operations and national economies. There is another transformation however that has been happening in the developed world over the last 25 years and now has the potential to bring sustainable development to the Global South in a way that was perhaps unthinkable just a few years ago. Just as the 4IR is impacting across the whole economic, social and cultural fabric of nations, so the rise of the digital-creative industries is leading the creative transformation of economies and societies in what we might call the Second Creative Revolution, or 2CR. One might also see this era then as something of a Second Renaissance.

The original Renaissance had its genesis in Italy in the fourteenth century and lasted for around three centuries. It is most often recognised as a creative and intellectual revival, an outpouring of cultural and critical thinking, of artistic and literary accomplishment from artists, writers and scientists such as Da Vinci, Michelangelo, Chaucer, Copernicus and Machiavelli. This explosion of creative thinking however also triggered a hugely innovative period, with impacts across the whole of society sparking a rise in the study of the sciences of astronomy, anatomy, mathematics and medicine.

The Renaissance led to the transformation of the economic system of Western Europe, moving from the feudal system of the medieval era, one based primarily on barter, to one based on market capitalism and the use of money. Innovations in communications, both written in terms of the birth and spread of printing, and physical innovations through better ship design and navigational instruments saw ideas and goods traded more widely than ever. Production methods and materials science saw the expansion of manufacturing in metals and textiles, and the early forms of mass production and specialisation began to emerge.

This new money economy saw the expansion of banking, the growth of towns into larger and more prosperous conurbations and the start of a migration of people from rural regions to these new centres of commerce, art and knowledge. The old social systems began to blur as this rise in trade and money exchange saw the rise of a new merchant middle class that then supported the pursuit of knowledge and the appreciation and commissioning of art through patronage. This explosion of innovation and societal change was born out of the creative and critical thinking that characterised Renaissance Italy and then spread to the developing economies of Northern Europe, having an equally significant impact on those countries.

The parallels of that revolution to the upheavals of today are certainly notable. The rise of the creative and cultural industries, powered by new digital technologies and platforms, has impacted the whole global economy, creating opportunities for entrepreneurs to reach new markets and leading to an explosion of creative and cultural production. However, we have to emphasise a note of caution in terms of the democratisation of this creative and technological explosion. Chapter 3 outlined how the impending negative impacts of 4IR on developing countries are becoming clear, with increasingly uneven development a distinctly plausible scenario for strategic planners in global financial and non-governmental institutions (Herweijer et al., 2018).

The role of education and innovation

Addressing this spatial imbalance then requires the actions of all key national and international actors, but at its heart is the role that education must play. The creative and technological disruptions that characterised the Renaissance are being mirrored in the challenges and opportunities we face today, with these industries offering the chance to create real sustainable growth but also enabling those richer, entrepreneurial frontier economies to move further away economically from the rest of the world.

The answer to this is to recognise that education, in all its forms, has to reform, innovate and engage with this new creative revolution.

National education policy in many developing as well as developed countries focuses on the STEM skills of science, technology, engineering and maths, with many schools scaling back the resources they dedicate to creative and cultural learning and knowledge. This is then failing to address the concern that the education system is unprepared for the changing nature of work. The STEAM concept of adding art into the equation is unfortunately simply a mechanism to add creativity, a little tokenistically, into the mix rather that realising that the whole STEM/STEAM concept needs fundamental rethinking.

If this is the case in developed countries and regions, where the digital-creative economy is generally more advanced and recognised, then the situation in small island states and other developing regions is far more challenging. Education, at primary, secondary, tertiary and professional levels, has to engage fully with this changing landscape, so rather than looking at the STEM/STEAM system to develop the skills required for the 4IR, we perhaps need one that focuses not on subjects but on approaches.

In responding to the WEF report, the acronym we use should perhaps be C3 – Creative, Critical and Cognitive. Creative is the common thread, much like digital, that is starting to run through every sector at every level. The pace of innovation is increasing, and without C3 skills to seed that innovation, regions and nations will become further distanced from the growth curve of the leading countries.

The ability of this new educational approach to engage in the Agile Helix concept discussed in Chapter 5 then offers the best opportunity to develop island entrepreneurship and build strong digital-creative ecosystems that will be the foundation of sustainable island economies. For SIDS, the fragility of their current economies is where a remodelled education approach, coupled to the opportunities of the 4IR and 2CR, can have their most significant impacts, enabling these countries and regions to become more active players in their own development (Roberts, 2018).

Routes to resilience for SIDS economies

Despite the challenges, there are, however, some positive examples of action being taken on the ground in the Caribbean, and in many ways, this region is leading the way in promoting creative economy development for SIDS.

The Branson Centre for Entrepreneurship, established in Jamaica in 2011, has become the region's leading start-up and business accelerator. Crucially, and uniquely for a SIDS region, it has developed a strong investment pipeline, allowing each entrepreneur cohort access to venture capital, with creative and cultural industries focused start-ups featuring strongly in the current accelerator programme.

Alongside this, the Caribbean Development Bank launched the Creative and Cultural Industries Investment Fund in 2017 as a way of stimulating growth in these key sectors, with an initial capitalisation of US$2.6 million. Importantly, this is grant funding for the creative sector and not debt funding, which so often is the default position for many MSME development funding schemes. The fund has also been able to support the creative sector's loss of revenue through the Covid-19 pandemic with emergency relief grants, a hugely positive action for a SIDS region.

These two development programmes demonstrate an awareness of the importance of the creative economy and a process whereby the sector can be supported and the entrepreneurship ecosystem developed.

In the Maldives, Sparkhub was launched in 2018 as a partnership between local entrepreneurs, with the aim of building and supporting the country's start-up ecosystem. It now works in collaboration with telecoms provider Dhiraagu and US accelerator Techstars to run Startup Weekends, as well as hackathons and ideas camps.

In Seychelles, the establishment of the Creative Industries National Events Agency (CINEA) in 2016 was a positive step, but there is a need to support CINEA with research, education and finance to deliver on its mandate. Again, and similar to strategies in the Caribbean, the creative industries have to be supported across all sectors and not just seen as carnivals and live events.

So why are these, albeit limited, examples not being recognised in wider strategic policy and research documents? In discussions around the sustainable development of small island states, why are these instances of good practice and positive impact not forming a more central part of the discussion? The reason may be that there is a seeming disconnect between individual creative industries projects such as those above and the broader research community, national government policy making, and international organisations. High quality research and data play a vitally important role here. Reliable and timely data is essential for strategy and decision-making at regional, national and international levels. Unfortunately there is a significant gap in the availability of reliable, high-quality data sets and contextualised analytics around the creative industries in small island states, as well as the wider developing world (UNCTAD Creative Economy Outlook, 2018).

As expressed in earlier chapters, this inevitably leads to research being based on outdated or very limited and possibly unreliable sources, strategic direction not reflecting the current state of economic, social and cultural reality, and hence policy making being out of step with real sustainable development needs and innovations.

This gap between research, data and policy has to be addressed so that island nations can make the best strategic decisions for their own sustainable development. There has been, and continues to be, an externalisation to sustainable development in SIDS, something that is driven from the outside by the major global actors and institutions, a process based on the fact that these small states lack the fiscal, institutional and technical instruments to be able to drive their development from within.

The purpose of developing the digital-creative industries in the regions, of enabling strong education, entrepreneurialism and innovation infrastructures in SIDS, is so that they can be the driver of this process and take ownership of their own sustainable development. This is a case not of retreating from international partnerships, far from it, but of reframing the methods by which they are conceived and implemented, the parameters that are set for these projects and the alignment of the projected outcomes to local conditions and needs.

There are some key steps to making this happen:

a) It is important that international organisations such as the UN are properly funded. The financial difficulties that UN departments such as UNESCO and UNCTAD face need to be addressed if the global cooperation required to support growth in SIDS, and more broadly to deliver on the decade of action, is actually to be facilitated and implemented. Major corporations also have an important role here in supporting, both financially and logistically, the work of the UNDP, for example, in its essential role with SIDS.

b) There needs to be reform in how these large-scale projects are designed and implemented. As has been discussed in earlier chapters, the SDGs, whilst primarily seen as a responsibility of national government, can actually only be made concrete by putting the private sector at the heart of the process. All development organisations have to make much greater use of innovators, entrepreneurs and SMEs if this is to happen.

c) There needs to be more research into the digital-creative sectors in SIDS, particularly their needs, gaps and opportunities. This must be applied and industry-focused research, conducted in partnership with island entrepreneurs, MSMEs, governments and development agencies. This will result in a greater depth of the contemporary, targeted and applicable data that will be essential in strategic thinking and policy making.

d) Encouraging non-debt investment in island entrepreneurship in the key digital-creative and knowledge-based sectors. The development of MSMEs in these sectors will be crucial to the sustainable development in island nations and central to this is access to finance to support innovation, start-ups, scale-ups and the support structures required. Whilst debt is an important element of this and is in part already available, VC, angel and private equity investment opportunities lag significantly behind. The structure needed for developing this island entrepreneurship can be understood as a progressive movement from one stage to the next and requires investment and support at each stage.

This entrepreneurship flow can then be modelled as a four-stage progression and defined as education–innovation–acceleration–monetisation. This encompasses the encouragement of creative and critical thinking in the formal education system that leads onto the generation of idea and innovations, which can, in turn, be supported through the mentoring and early stage development of products in accelerator programmes, finally leading onto seed investment in start-up MSMEs and the commercialisation and monetisation of those digital-creative products.

These actions then have the possibility of addressing the lack of progress on the SDGs but can only be understood and implemented if all partners in their delivery can look critically at their own strategies and structures. The case for this is as pressing as it has ever been.

Global hunger has risen for the third year in a row, the digital gender gap is widening, not narrowing, and less than 5% of countries are on track to meet childhood obesity and tuberculosis targets (Fullman et al., 2017). We've seen how the increased exploitation of ocean resources and environments as part of the Blue Economy strategy has been increasing acidification and biodiversity loss. This trade-off between one SDG and another is a common problem and shows a lack of coordinated and cross-sector and multi-sector thinking.

These contradictions can be seen across the SDGs in the real world and the offered solutions, whilst suggesting some positive action, ironically possess the same compartmentalised approach as the action on specific SDGs. Greater global cooperation is often stated as a route forward, which is of course positive, but then this cooperation is envisaged as simply more researchers and policy makers coming together to discuss the situation.

If the next ten years are to see any real progress at all, then innovation has to be at the centre of the process, and no more so than in the organisations entrusted with the delivery of these goals. We have to look at radical solutions, and this starts with the whole way in which we think about the delivery mechanisms of the SDGs.

The creative economy as the foundation of sustainable growth for SIDS

The challenge of transforming the global trade and growth model away from the current polluting, waste-producing and damaging production and consumption model to one that is not just sustainable but environmentally positive is undoubtedly the greatest test we face over the next 20 years. We have no option to go back, no matter what pre-industrial utopian vision is wished for, as the planet's growing population demands we find new ways to not just feed and house them but give everyone the secure and rewarding quality of life they deserve. That means finding new economic models, not in the political sense, but in the dynamics of innovation and commercialisation.

Nowhere are these challenges greater than in SIDS, but as we've seen in previous chapters, the models of intervention, support and partnership have had mixed success.

The issues facing SIDS can certainly only be addressed through global partnerships and concerted and collaborative actions. However, SIDS themselves must be an active participant of that process. The international collaborative action focused on SIDS has to look at how the internal challenges they face can be addressed, how the structures and ecosystems of education and entrepreneurship can be developed, and how these can then lead the process of dealing with the vulnerabilities so often cited as the focus of external interventions.

Little has been done to address these internal needs in any consistent or strategic way. Instead, funding and expertise have come from outside to deliver specific sectoral projects and interventions, and whilst valuable, this process inevitably just perpetuates the notion that sustainable development is something that is 'done to' rather than being 'done with' SIDS. Why can climate, clean energy, healthcare or ocean innovations not be driven by the very states where they impact the most and by the people who probably understand them, in a real sense, better than anyone else?

Whilst this is far from an easy fix, what the digital-creative industries can do is set the educational and innovation foundations that SIDS can use to build skills and talent and then crucially retain that talent. They offer the most effective way of engaging an often disengaged youth whose lack of opportunity beyond the hospitality or public sectors leads to disaffection and social problems. The 4IR and the 2CR offer the opportunity to build an economy based on digital, creative, technological skills, innovation, entrepreneurialism and sustainable growth.

Creative innovation extends far beyond what is normally perceived as the creative industries and into every sector of the global economy. Look at the impacts of immersive content production on the construction and healthcare sectors, of digital storytelling on tourism and democracy and of creative thinking in corporate governance and leadership.

The creative economy is the new powerhouse of the global economy. Creative industries, heritage and culture are no longer something that is 'nice to do'. They are the single fastest-growing industry sector, driven by the new digital industrial revolution and the ubiquity of cheap technology for consumption. This creative revolution is rapidly becoming a central part of every other sector, adding value through content, visualisations, products, services and technologies. The relationship between digital content, technology platforms, cultural production and consumption is increasing in scale and reach, disrupting financial services, healthcare, tourism, construction and education. This revolution is developing a creative thread that links innovation, technology and culture to the new potential of every commercial sector.

So for SIDS, whose economies are traditionally narrow and based around the oceans, the digital-creative sector offers the possibility not just of opening up new sources or jobs, growth and prosperity but of becoming the real foundation of the innovation required across the whole of their economic structures. This is a case not of replacing one with the other but of recognising that a strong digital-creative economy can support the Blue Economy, take pressure of the exploitation of the oceans and create a more equal, diverse engaged economy.

There are some key pillars to achieving this.

SIDS have to develop a 'mixed economy' of creative and cultural institutions, SMEs, education and finance partners and an informed and flexible policy landscape. This will fuel a thriving creative innovation and enterprise environment where creative and traditional sectors such as those of the Blue Economy can collaborate and see the benefits of 'creative spillovers'.

SIDS will need to develop a business support framework that optimises the take-up of existing enterprise, investment and employment support amongst creative businesses and looks for investment to provide more tailored and expert programmes that meet the specific needs that generic programmes do not offer.

The development of the Creative, Critical and Cognitive (C3) education system at secondary, tertiary and professional levels will provide the learning and skills continuum so crucial to building and maintaining relevant and up-to-date skills and competencies. It will also widen participation in the creative economy and gradually build the strength of the skills base.

Reimagining the possible scale of the creative economy in developing regions and small island states from a research, policy and strategic point is essential. Too often the creative economy as a large-scale producer of products, jobs and GDP is spatially restricted. Consumers, small-scale producers and pockets of excellence are increasingly global, but investment in and recognition of the creative economy as a central driver of growth is certainly not. Whilst many countries have the creative and cultural industries in their '2030 growth strategies', the translation of this to action and investment is often not followed through, subordinate as it so often is to traditional manufacturing or technology sectors.

Moving the creative economy up the policy agenda for SIDS then requires researchers, the private sector and international organisations to recognise its value, engage in its growth and collaborate in connected innovation. By doing that, island states have the possibility of changing their whole narrative and writing a different future.

Beyond vulnerability: the goal of the creative island state

The narrative of vulnerability that often surrounds discussion of SIDS, whilst undoubtedly based on concrete realities, must not become all-pervasive and must be countered by strategies and actions based on applied research, solid data and an awareness that changing trade models around digital technologies are just as relevant to SIDS as they are to the world's leading economies. The same sectors, innovations and advances that are powering the developed world can also equally apply to island states.

So the weight of literature and consequent strategic decision-making around climate impacts, ocean degradation, over-tourism and the need for heavy investment in the Blue Economy to offset these effects is overlooking the importance of innovation, human resource development and trade in these digital-creative sectors. It is also underestimating the potential for developing knowledge-based, creative local economies that, thanks to the impact of the rapidly advancing technologies of production and distribution, allow these traditionally isolated regions to insert themselves into the new global digital trade market.

The roll-out of 5G capabilities in Seychelles with the investment from Intelvision, alongside its aim of 95% coverage and significantly greater smartphone penetration, will open up notable opportunities for entrepreneurs, innovators and creators to move into global digital export markets.

Resilience therefore for SIDS is a case not just of science and technology mitigating the effects of climate change or developing new clean-energy sources but of framing sustainable development for these regions as encompassing all aspects of economy, society, culture, innovation and government. Whilst the challenges of limited land area and domestic markets, finite resources, physical isolation from global markets and increased transport costs are all correct, accepting them as the reason for low levels of creative entrepreneurship is reductionist and no longer holds entirely true.

More important areas of action today for small island states have been discussed in the previous chapters and present a roadmap forward for SIDS. Increasing the flows of FDI in sectors other than tourism and infrastructure, building better and more collaborative R&D capability, implementing more favourable local finance terms for MSMEs, enabling a better private sector business environment to encourage investors and creating a more educationally engaged youth that can then lead to a modern, high-skill and high-wage workforce are the crucial areas for action.

These are certainly not insignificant barriers, but they are also not insurmountable. SIDS cannot change their geographical characteristics, so reiterating those as a reason for an assumed irreversibly narrow and fragile economy is not appropriate. Instead, the focus should be on creating a knowledge-based economy and supporting this through the educational, business, technology, fiscal, investment and regulatory environments that allow island peoples to create, innovate, build value in their ideas and content and then monetise these through the rapid digital transformation of the global market.

The innovative thinking that saw the Seychelles create the world's first sovereign blue bond cannot just be restricted to the Blue Economy. Let's take that innovation and use it to build a strong, resilient and sustainable twenty-first-century digital-creative economy for island states that is inclusive, equitable and supports the health of our ocean environments and the creative ambitions of its peoples.

References

Fullman, N., et al. 2017. Measuring Progress and Projecting Attainment on the Basis of Past Trends of the Health-Related Sustainable Development Goal in 188 Countries: An Analysis from the Global Burden of Disease Study 2016. *The Lancet*, 390(10100), pp. 1423–1459.

Herweijer, C., Combes, B., Johnson, L., McCargow, R., Bhardwaj, S., Jackson, B. & Ramchandani, P. 2018. Enabling a Sustainable Fourth Industrial Revolution: How G20

Countries Can Create the Conditions for Emerging Technologies to Benefit People and the Planet (No. 2018–32). Economics Discussion Papers.

Roberts, J.L. 2018. Small Island Developing States and Sustainable Development Goals: Curse or Cure. In *Handbook of Small State*, pp. 517–529. Routledge, London.

United Nations Conference on Trade and Development. 2018. *Creative Economy Outlook: Trends in International Trade in Creative Industries*. UNCTAD, Geneva. Accessed at https://unctad.org/en/pages/publicationswebflyer.aspx?publicationid=2328.

World Economic Forum. 2018. *The Future of Jobs Report, 2018*. WEF, Geneva. Accessed at www.weforum.org/reports/the-future-of-jobs-report-2018.

Index

Note: Page numbers in *italics* indicate a figure on the corresponding page.